W9-ATQ-866

THE COMPASSION
OF DOGS

KIM D.R. DEARTH

The

COMPASSION
of DOGS

⁓

HEARTWARMING STORIES

OF LOYALTY AND KINDNESS

Prima Publishing

Copyright © 2002 by Prima Publishing, a division of
Random House, Inc.

Published by Prima Publishing, Roseville, California. Member of the
Crown Publishing Group, a division of Random House, Inc.

PRIMA PUBLISHING and colophon are trademarks of Random
House, Inc., registered with the United States Patent and Trademark
Office.

Library of Congress Cataloging-in-Publication Data
Dearth, Kim.
    The compassion of dogs : heartwarming stories of loyalty and
kindness / Kim D.R. Dearth.
      p.   cm.
    ISBN 0-7615-3590-X
    1. Dogs—Anecdotes. 2. Dog owners—Anecdotes. 3. Human-
animal relationships—Anecdotes. I. Title.
SF426.2 .D42   2002
636.7—dc21   2002070520

02 03 04 05 AA 10 9 8 7 6 5 4 3 2 1
Printed in the United States of America

First Edition

Visit us online at www.primapublishing.com

*This book is dedicated to my husband, Dave,
and my son, Dylan, who are my greatest supporters,
and to my Shetland Sheepdog, Rio,
who is my constant companion.*

CONTENTS

FOREWORD

As a reporter and broadcaster, I've written and spoken on TV and radio about the amazing things dogs can do. But what's most amazing to me is that even though people have lived side by side with dogs for thousands of years, we seem to know so little about them. And yet, at the same time, they seem to know so much about us.

Case in point: The Chicago-based animal assisted therapy (AAT) group called the Chenny Troupe. The Chenny Troupe dogs and their volunteers participate in what's called goal directed therapy. The idea is to achieve therapeutic goals as directed by the medical staff. For example, as a part of AAT, or canine rehab, a stroke victim might be asked to grip and then ultimately succeed in tossing a tennis ball to a retriever. I've seen Chenny Troupe dogs achieve miracles time and again as they somehow reach deep into a person's soul, locating a place where medical professionals and even family members can't get to.

My wife, Robin, and our dog, Lucy, have volunteered with the group for the past five years. During one of her weekly sessions, she walked into the Rehabilitation Institute of Chicago to find a little boy seated in a wheelchair. The little boy smiled just like Mike when Robin asked for a high five. She didn't have to ask the question, "So, you're a basketball fan?" The scrawny 11-year-old was lost inside a Michael Jordan Bulls jersey.

Robin was told that the little boy, named Jerold, had had surgery that impacted the use of his vocal cords. According to group leader Judy Keitz, "Jerold can talk, he's just afraid to say much and he's very afraid to speak with any volume." Robin was instructed that her goal was to have Jerold call Lucy to him from about five feet.

Robin took our dog Lucy and walked over to Jerold. He began to cringe in fear. It occurred to Robin, why would anyone who is terrified of dogs call one? So she stopped a few feet away. Lucy, a 24-pound North American Shepherd (Miniature Australian Shepherd), looked to Jerold, summed up the situation, and let out a loud "whahoo!" At fist the boy jumped in his chair from fright, but before he could get too scared, Lucy was rolling over and over and over. She continued her act of whahoo-ing and rolling over again and again. Before long, Jerold couldn't help himself and began to laugh. This was Robin's opening, and she took it.

Robin explained to Jerold, "See, she wants you to pet her tummy." Within minutes Jerold was actually petting

Lucy. When Robin asked if he wanted Lucy to roll over again, Jerold shook his head "yes." Knowing that the goal was for Jerold to use his voice, Robin replied, "You have to tell her in your loudest voice."

Jerold's voice was weak the first time he said, "Lucy, roll over." But Lucy complied, and Jerold laughed again. He was having fun, but he also felt empowered. Within minutes, Jerold was rattling off all sorts of commands to Lucy. "Lucy, sit." "Lucy, lay down." And each time, Robin gently cajoled, "Just a little louder, now, so Lucy can hear you." By the end of the session, Jerold was actually calling out clearly from the other side of the gymnasium-sized room, "Lucy, come!"

On the following Wednesday, the moment Lucy appeared, Jerold called out, "Lucy, come!" She bolted toward him, pulling the leash right from Robin's hand. After exhausting Lucy with a series of "Lucy, come!" commands, Robin suggested that Jerold let the little pooch rest. Lucy sat in a chair next to Jerold's. As he petted her, Robin overheard Jerold sharing a secret with his new canine friend: "My family is upstairs watching the Bulls game, but I decided I'd rather be here with you." This was major; Jerold was actually missing a Bulls *playoff* game.

Robin and Lucy saw Jerold for two more consecutive Wednesdays. On the third Wednesday, Lucy and Robin entered the room where the dogs work, but this time no one called out Lucy's name. The therapist came up to Robin with tears in her eyes. Robin was thinking the worst as the therapist hugged her. "Jerold went home. It's a month earlier than we expected," she said. "I'm absolutely certain if it wasn't for Lucy, Jerold would still be struggling."

In *Compassion of Dogs,* Kim Dearth describes similarly amazing tales. She describes dogs who predict seizures, real-life Lassies who have saved lives or rescued lost people, and the dogs who worked as tirelessly as any of the other heroic rescue workers on the scene following the terrorists attacks of September 11.

I wish I could explain how Lucy connected with Jerold when mere humans could not. Or how dogs can predict seizures, or how they think about saving lives even if it means putting their own at risk. But I can't. It has been scientifically proven that AAT works. You may not get a chance to peruse the numbers and statistics in the veterinary and psychology journals that have finally begun to document what dogs can do, but you can read this book to find stories about real-life folks who have been touched by a canine angel. I do have one caveat: This book should be rated T, for tissues. Before you dive in, grab a box. You'll need some.

We're only beginning to understand the depth and potential impact of the human-animal bond. *The Compassion of Dogs* is an excellent start.

—STEVE DALE

ACKNOWLEDGMENTS

To an author, every book is like a child. It is conceived with the tiniest of ideas, then grows with each sentence, until the day it is ready for the "birth" of the printing press. While each book holds a special place in my heart, this one has truly been a labor of love.

Although I knew I would gather many interesting stories while writing this book, I never imagined how these stories would touch my life. I feel a profound connection to all the people who related their stories to me. I shared laughter and tears with many of the people who contributed to this book, and I grieved with some of them as they told me of the loss of their precious companions. I want to thank them all for opening up their hearts and allowing me to tell their special stories.

I also would like to thank the wonderful organizations that helped me gather these stories, including Delta

Society, Therapy Dogs International, Paws With a Cause, Canine Companions for Independence, and Hearing Dogs for Deaf People. A special thank you to my father, Dick Ruhl, who took it upon himself to hunt down stories for me as well.

And, finally, I would like to thank my husband, Dave, who is my greatest fan and promoter, my son, Dylan, who brings joy and meaning to my life every day, and my family, both biological and in-law, who have always provided encouragement and loving support. And, of course, a special thank you to Rio, Gorby, and Tux, the furry friends who demonstrate the compassion of animals in my own life.

INTRODUCTION

When I was first approached to write this book, I was thrilled. I've loved animals, especially dogs, since I was 5 years old and declared to my parents that I was going to be a veterinarian. While I chose a slightly different path, that of journalism, I never gave up my passion for animals.

I was also fascinated by the concept of compassion. While many scientists debate whether animals have emotions, every animal lover I know would vehemently argue that they do, and each has countless stories to back up his or her beliefs. In fact, a number of scientists have recently found evidence that animals do indeed experience similar emotions to humans—those of love, loyalty, and yes, compassion.

I had one nagging question going into this project, however. That was the question of my own dog's compassion.

While I knew that Rio, my Shetland Sheepdog, loved me, he never showed the compassion of many other dogs. He would follow me from room to room, lie at my feet while I worked at my computer, and was always up for a walk around the neighborhood or a game of Frisbee in the backyard. But he didn't seem very in tune with my feelings. If I cried or was visibly upset about something, he basically ignored me. I would joke to my husband that Rio had the sensitivity of a rock!

Then several weeks before this project was due, I noticed a drastic change in Rio's demeanor toward me. While he always followed me around when I was doing laundry or cleaning, now he followed so closely that he bumped into me if I stopped abruptly. When I asked him what was wrong, he looked at me with soulful, worried eyes and leaned against my legs. He was with me in the kitchen, the bedroom, and the bathroom. He even stood outside the tub staring until I reappeared from behind the shower curtain every morning.

Rio is a fairly independent dog who normally lies on the couch with me for a few minutes until his fluffy fur makes him too hot and he jumps down to find a cooler spot on the floor. Now, however, he would jump up next to me in the evenings and remain there for as long as I sat, panting audibly, but refusing to leave until I moved first.

I thought there must be something wrong with him. I took him to two different veterinarians, but they could find nothing. They asked if there were any new stresses in his life. The second vet even remarked that Rio looked visibly depressed. But I could think of nothing new that was causing him such worry.

This went on for several weeks and I began to ignore Rio's actions, thinking that whatever was bothering him would go away and he would revert to normal. But every time I turned around, he was underfoot, pleading with his eyes.

Then, a week before my deadline, I felt a sharp pain in my chest. It went away and I ignored it. I had too much to do to worry about a little discomfort. The pain came and went for several days, until one day, it seared through like a knife piercing my rib cage. I lay down but this time the pain didn't go away. By that evening, I was huddled in a ball on the couch, shivering with a 103° fever. All the while, Rio never left my side. When I decided to sleep on the couch for the night, Rio leaped up and curled in the crook of my legs, only jumping down to accompany me on trips to the bathroom to splash cool water on my face.

The next morning, I made a doctor's appointment. A chest x-ray confirmed the doctor's suspicions. I had a serious case of pneumonia. When I returned home, Rio resumed his post beside me on the couch. I hugged him tightly. Had he sensed my illness, sensed the fluid building up in my lungs? I truly believe he did. I chided myself for ever doubting his compassion.

In the pages of this book, you'll find more miraculous stories of dogs showing compassion in their relationships with people and even other animals. You'll meet Endal, who covered his wheelchair-bound owner with a blanket, brought him his cell phone, and barked for help when his owner was struck by a hit-and-run driver. You'll meet Tiffany, who virtually taught herself to be a hearing dog for a young man who was deaf, and twice saved the man's mother when she collapsed due to diabetic shock. And, you'll meet the dogs of September 11—from the search and rescue canines who toiled tirelessly to find the victims of the horrible attack on the World Trade Center, to a therapy dog who brought comfort to the human workers and victim's families who needed it most.

I hope you'll be as touched by their testaments as I was. Their tales are proof that compassion is not solely a human emotion.

CHAPTER I

DOGS AS CAREGIVERS

Since the very first wolf ventured close to the fire and forged a relationship with early humans, people and dogs have depended upon each other. Although some dogs still perform traditional tasks such as hunting and herding, dogs with these skills are now more often used for sport rather than out of any real need for their skills. Still, dogs seem to possess an inherent need to help people. Many dogs fill this need by working as assistance dogs for the blind, deaf, disabled, and mentally ill.

Most people are familiar with the duties of the guide dog, who serves as eyes for his blind master. Less familiar, but just as important, are hearing dogs, assistance dogs, and psychiatric service dogs. Hearing dogs are trained to alert their owners to sounds such as a ringing doorbell, a stove timer, or a smoke alarm and then lead their owner to the source of the sound or indicate that there is danger. Assistance dogs are trained for a variety of duties, including picking up a dropped object, pulling a wheelchair, placing laundry in a washing machine, and pushing an elevator button. Psychiatric service dogs, perhaps the least known of all types of caregiver dogs, help their owners cope with mental conditions such as bipolar disorder (manic depression) and agoraphobia (fear of leaving the house). They do this by showing unconditional love and helping their owner remain grounded and focused on the task at hand.

Some may argue that these dogs are just well-trained animals. But dogs are not forced into service. In fact, a dog that does not display the proper temperament and willingness to learn during his training program will not pass the program and will, instead, be adopted out as a pet. Assistance dogs are noted for their eagerness; they learn each new task with unbridled enthusiasm. This compassion is especially evident in dogs such as Tiffany, whom you will meet in this chapter, who was not officially trained to be a hearing dog but instead sensed her owner's disability and figured out how best to help him cope.

Thanks to organizations such as Seeing Eye Guide Dogs for the Blind, Canine Companions for Independence, Paws With a Cause, and countless others, dogs receive the training to enhance what they have done naturally since the beginning of time—assist their human companions.

PATRA

When Donna Jacobs of Lohman, Missouri, suffered a stroke in 1994, her world was turned upside down. Donna, who was a greeting card designer at the time of the stroke, had always been a creative person, but now she couldn't tap into that creativity. She felt she had been robbed of her identity. In addition, she experienced ongoing seizures as a result of the stroke. Her memory often failed her, and her cognitive skills were diminished. "Sometimes I would say I was hot when I was cold," says Donna.

She fell into a severe depression and isolated herself at her rural home. After two years, her husband, John, was willing to try anything to help his wife. When he heard of puppies being given away in a nearby town, he suggested they take a look. Donna and John returned home with not one, but two six-week-old Rottweiler/German Shepherd mixes. Donna chose the female, Cleo, for her own, while Patra, the male, became John's dog.

The Jacobs soon discovered that the puppies were flea-infested and suffered from internal parasites. Caring for the dogs forced Donna to get out of bed every morning, and she began to focus on nursing the puppies back to health rather than thinking about her own ailments.

At four months, Cleo no longer had the strength to fight, and she died. The dog's death set Donna back emotionally, and she once again pulled away from the world around her. She refused to leave home, withdrew from family and friends, and even locked the door when a caregiver arrived to provide nursing assistance. The only activity she allowed herself was gardening.

Around the time that Cleo died, Patra began acting differently toward Donna. She and John had taken Patra through puppy obedience classes, and although he performed flawlessly to John's commands, he ignored

Donna's. Donna was still experiencing seizures, so she spent a lot of time in her garden near the house where she felt safe. While she worked, Patra would come up to Donna and head butt her, nip at her sweatpants, and knock her to the ground. Then he would stand over her, preventing her from getting up. The more she yelled at him, the more excited he became. While she was on the ground, the 35-pound, 5-month-old puppy would continue to head butt her and nip at her ears.

Donna wondered whether Patra's behavior was a reaction to Cleo's death, or whether it was caused by something else. Although Patra never showed severe aggression, Donna and John decided to take him to the veterinarian to have him neutered, hoping this would calm him down. When the vet told them she felt Patra was too young to be neutered, Donna was convinced she needed to find the dog a new home. The vet noticed the bite marks and bruises on Donna's arms and ears, which curiously were restricted to her left side. The vet suggested that before giving up, the Jacobs contact a dog trainer who had just moved to the area.

Kathy Cramer, a service dog trainer with Assistance Dogs for Living and a certified canine behaviorist, visited Donna and Patra in their home. She asked Donna to go about her normal tasks while she watched. She observed Patra knock Donna down as he had before, then she watched Patra interact with John. Although Patra was a canine angel with John, he refused to listen to Donna's commands. Kathy asked Donna to keep a journal of Patra's misbehavior and to turn her back on him and ignore him whenever he acted up.

When Kathy returned two weeks later, nothing had changed. Donna said she had tried ignoring the dog, but he persisted in knocking her down. Kathy asked Donna to continue keeping the journal, but this time to record what was happening with herself every time Patra misbehaved. John agreed to observe and help Donna record the events surrounding Patra's behavior.

The next time Patra acted up, Donna called John to come watch. They were in the living room. For the first time, Donna didn't fight Patra off and instead laid down on the floor. Patra immediately stopped his misbehavior and laid down next to Donna on her left side, resting his paws on her arm and laying his head on her shoulder. Donna felt her heart palpitate and her breathing become shallow. She was barely aware of Patra licking the left side of her face, neck and mouth, then her awareness trailed off. When she came to, she asked John what had happened. Dumbfounded, John told her; Patra had alerted to her seizure.

The next time Kathy visited, she told Donna to reward Patra's behavior by lying down. Patra soon learned to curtail his nipping and use of force, and instead began to put his paws in her lap and gently nudge Donna with his head when he sensed a seizure coming on.

"Patra gave me more than any human could," says Donna. Knowing that Patra would warn her of an oncoming seizure and stay by her side through its duration convinced Donna that she could go out in public without fear. "Because of him, I regained the confidence and self-esteem to get a job and rejoin society."

When Donna landed a job as marketing director for a computer company, Patra accompanied her to work every day. If he indicated a seizure was imminent, Donna hung a "Do Not Disturb" sign on the door until the seizure had passed.

Although Donna enjoyed her job, she felt Patra was showing her another calling in life. She quit her job to found a nonprofit organization called Service Dogs Today that helps disabled people with limited income pay for their assistance dogs' equipment and training. The organization also uses veterinarians and groomers to educate owners about proper nutrition and grooming of service dogs. It also provides information on service dog access laws. Currently, Donna is working to help pass a new service dog bill in the state of Missouri to improve public awareness and access.

Having Patra by her side has greatly reduced the number of seizures Donna has experienced. She also discovered that Patra could often sense health conditions in others. He once alerted to Donna's former boss' high blood pressure and has predicted impending epileptic seizures of fellow attendees at service dog conventions. Patra was recognized for his incredible ability and service in 1998 when he was named Delta Society's Service Dog of the Year.

Still, Patra's foremost concern is Donna. One day, after visiting the dentist, Donna returned to work but felt weak and sluggish. Patra began to head butt her, then nipped at the buttons on her blouse, something he had never done before. When Donna called his trainer, Kathy, to relate what he was doing, she told Donna to get to the hospital immediately. When she arrived, an EKG and ultrasound revealed Donna had an infection in the pulmonary valve of her heart.

"This dog has saved my life twice," says Donna. "He not only alerts me when I'm going to seizure, but he also helps me deal with anxiety attacks. It is incredibly soothing just to be able to put my hands on him, stroke him, and know I'm not alone. I wouldn't be where I am today if it wasn't for Patra."

TIFFANY

We've all heard stories of dogs who have "picked" their owners. Occasionally, a puppy totters away from his littermates to crawl into a potential owner's lap and shower her with doggie kisses, as if to say, "No need to look any further—I'm the one for you." Or sometimes a stray appears on the doorstep of someone who is grieving the loss of a recently departed pet, yet has been afraid to welcome a new companion into his heart. Sometimes a dog even shows an uncanny ability to sense a potential partner's unique need and decides to take it upon herself to meet that need.

Joyce Hansen, a Shetland Sheepdog breeder in Gervais, Oregon, tells of one dog who not only chose her owner, but who also figured out how to make his life more livable.

One day, Joyce received a call from a woman who wanted to bring her son out to take a look at Joyce's Shelties. Mrs. Halter explained that Tim was deaf. He had lost his job and didn't have many friends or go out much. He was plagued with low self-esteem. Tim had applied for a hearing dog with an organization that places such dogs, but his hopes were crushed when the organization turned down his application due to his living arrangements. Because he lived at home with other people, the personnel at the organization felt the dog would get confused and not be able to properly perform its duties. Mrs. Halter was desperate to find something to lift her son's spirits. She had heard Shelties were intelligent and easy to train. She hoped to find a puppy who would help her son.

Tim and his mother met every puppy Joyce had to offer. As they walked around Joyce's property looking at the dogs, Joyce noticed a canine shadow following them. A one-year-old female named Tiffany that Joyce had planned to keep was standing next to Tim. As they walked a little farther and continued their conversation, Joyce noticed that Tiffany never left Tim's side. Mrs. Halter noticed as well. Although she had been looking for a puppy, she asked if this dog was for sale. Joyce said no—Tiffany was perfect for the show ring and would make a wonderful addition to her breeding program. Mrs. Halter seemed disappointed, so Joyce said she would think about it, all the while knowing it would take a lot for her to give up this special dog.

Tim and his mother drove off, and Joyce headed back to the house. She noticed that Tiffany wasn't following. Instead, the dog stayed by the gate and watched the car as it pulled out of the driveway. One hour later, Joyce came out of the house to get something, and Tiffany was still sitting at the gate, waiting for Tim to come back. Two hours later, Tiffany was still waiting. Joyce says, "After three hours, I called Mrs. Halter and told her to come and pick up her son's dog. It was obvious I was being told he needed her more than I did."

Tim and his mother returned, and the Sheltie greeted him as if he were her long-lost owner, her whole body wiggling with delight. Although Joyce was sorry to see Tiffany go, she felt that she had done the right thing. A few weeks later, she was sure.

Mrs. Halter called and explained that a few minutes after they got home with Tiffany, the phone had rung. The Sheltie went to the phone and then to Tim, then back to the phone, as if to tell him there was something that needed his attention. At first Mrs. Halter thought it was just a coincidence—how could this dog possibly know that Tim couldn't hear? Maybe she just didn't like the noisy jangle of the phone and wanted someone to make it stop. But the phone rang again, and the Sheltie reacted the same way.

Over the next several weeks, Tiffany reacted the same way to the sound of the doorbell, the timer on the stove, and the fire alarm near the kitchen that was set off by an overcooked dinner. At each sound, Tiffany would race to Tim's side, bark and paw at him to get his attention, then rush back to whatever was causing the sound. She would continue running back and forth until Tim followed her to the source of the sound. Tim's mother asked Joyce how she had taught this dog to perform as a hearing dog, and why she hadn't told them that the dog was trained. Joyce was speechless; she had never trained Tiffany to perform any of these feats. This amazing little dog had sensed the young man's disability and had discovered on her own how to help the world communicate with him and, in turn, help him communicate back.

This in itself would be enough to prove Tiffany a remarkable dog, but the little Sheltie would turn out to be a hero not only to Tim, but to his mother as well.

One day, Mrs. Halter, who is diabetic, was in the kitchen cooking while Tim and his father were watching television in another room. Suddenly, Mrs. Halter's insulin dropped dramatically, and she fell to the floor. Too weak to move or even call out for help, she felt panic rising within her. She knew an attack like this could be fatal if she didn't receive treatment right away. Then, out of the corner of her eye, she saw a furry flash dart from the kitchen down the hallway. Tiffany raced to Tim's side barking frantically, then rushed back toward the kitchen. Tim and his father followed the dog and found Mrs. Halter lying on the floor. They called an ambulance and rushed Mrs. Halter to the hospital. Her insulin had dipped dangerously low, and the paramedics worked quickly in the ambulance to stabilize her. When they reached the hospital, doctors confirmed what the Halters had already known; Tiffany had saved Mrs. Halter's life.

Tiffany continued to live with the Halters for many years and came to the rescue one more time when Mrs. Halter experienced another attack. Tiffany also continued to perform smaller miracles every day, helping Tim cope with his disability and gain confidence to live in a hearing world.

Sadly, Tiffany's health deteriorated when she was twelve, and she was put to sleep in May 2001. Tim was devastated over the loss of Tiffany. Mrs. Halter knew no dog could fully replace Tiffany, but she also knew Tim needed another dog to help him heal. She called Joyce and explained what had happened.

Joyce immediately thought of a dog who reminded her of Tiffany. This Sheltie had difficulty getting pregnant, and Joyce felt the five-year-old dog might be better off as a pet rather than staying in the breeding program. When Tim showed up, Annie immediately ran to him and would not leave his side.

"It was like seeing Tiffany and Tim thirteen years ago," says Joyce. The Halters decided to take Annie, but they weren't able to bring her home that day. As Tim and his mother prepared to drive off, Tim reached out the car window to pet Annie good-bye. The Sheltie seemed to understand he couldn't reach her, so she leaped onto Joyce's leg to touch Tim's hand with her nose.

Joyce called to check on Annie's progress after the Sheltie had been with the Halters for six months. Although Annie wasn't as quick to adapt to Tim's needs as Tiffany had been, she was showing aptitude in being a hearing dog by jumping off Tim's lap and running toward the kitchen when she heard the timer go off. Mrs. Halter was sure it would only be a matter of time before Annie could fully take over Tiffany's duties as Tim's assistance dog.

Joyce says, "Annie seems to have the spirit of Tiffany with her. When the Halters picked Annie up, I told them I would be watching for another Sheltie like Tiffany and Annie in ten years or so." Even in death, Tiffany's spirit seems to live on, watching over the man she chose as her owner so many years ago.

SANDY

Becky Horowitz, LMSW-ACP, BCD, a clinical social worker, wrote to share a story about an amazing canine she met through her job at Hospice of VNA (Circle of Hope) in El Paso, Texas. She first met Sandy the Golden Retriever several years ago when Sandy's owner, Walter Chapman, was admitted for hospice care. Sandy was sitting by Walter's recliner and seemed to wonder about the reason for Becky's visit. After observing Becky for a few minutes, Sandy seemed to sense that she was there to help, and accepted Becky as a friend. This friendship grew as Sandy's owner's condition progressed.

Sandy rarely left her owner's side. When he was finally placed in a hospital bed, her station changed from her position adjacent to the chair to a new vantage point under the bed. She monitored everyone who came into the house, and seemed to sense that the hospice care team was there to help. She allowed the workers to touch and provide care for her owner, yet was always vigilant to ensure no harm came to her companion. Although she never so much as growled at a visitor, she expressed any doubts about a new health care provider by positioning herself between the new person and her owner. She lovingly became known as the hospice nurse with four legs.

Although Sandy shared her home with two younger dogs, her interaction with them was minimal. Her primary focus was to be close to and attentive to her owner, only leaving his side when it became necessary to eat or relieve herself. As Walter's condition worsened, the hospice workers' worries about Sandy grew. How would Sandy adjust once her owner was no longer with her?

The hospice care team's concerns were realized when Sandy's owner passed away. Sandy showed her grief by only eating when coaxed and expressing little interest in the activities around her. Soon after Walter's death, his widow, Dorothy, fell and broke her hip. Since Dorothy could no longer care for Sandy, the hospice social worker found Sandy a foster home with another hospice family. Although the family already owned two dogs, they opened their home and their hearts to the Golden.

Sandy's reaction to her new owner, Jay Sherwin, was almost immediate. She seemed to sense the need to resume her role of "nurse" and stationed herself close to him at all times. When he sat in his wheelchair, she would sit by his side, and when he was in bed, she lay down nearby. Occasionally, she would even crawl into bed with him, warming his body with her soft, abundant coat.

As Jay's condition worsened, Sandy became even more attentive, just as she had before. She showed little interest in playing with the other two dogs in the house. She simply would not allow herself to be a dog and engage in the usual canine games and activities. She seemed to have decided that her role was different from that of her canine companions—she was a caregiver, and she was determined to do this job well.

One day, Sandy rose to greet her owner, but her greeting wasn't returned. Sandy and Jay's wife, Rene, shared their grief, leaning on and comforting each other as only those who have experienced such a loss can. Although Sandy had been taken on as a foster dog, Rene officially adopted Sandy and welcomed her as a part of the family. Slowly, Sandy began to heal. Each day, she showed a little more interest in resuming normal activities, and even began to interact with her canine housemates.

Becky says, "It is now our joy to watch her frolicking in the yard with her younger canine siblings and chasing a ball when it is thrown. It is as if she has completed two missions and can now allow herself to be a dog. She has certainly earned this freedom and the respect of the hospice care team. If we had graded Sandy's job performance, she would have received an A+."

BARNABY

Barnaby serves as Marjorie's ears. Marjorie, who is deaf, was paired with Barnaby more than five years ago through Hearing Dogs for Deaf People, a charitable organization in the United Kingdom. This lovable, dark-eyed, Golden Retriever is invaluable to Marjorie around the house and workplace.

Barnaby is one of nearly a thousand hearing dogs in the United Kingdom who alert their owners to everyday sounds that hearing people often take for granted. There is no particular breed that works best as a hearing dog. Hearing Dogs for Deaf People prides itself on selecting dogs from rescue organizations and shelters throughout the country. These organizations are the charity's top source for well-behaved, trainable young dogs, followed closely by donated litters or unwanted pets. The Golden

Retriever Club rescued Barnaby as a six-month-old puppy and donated him to Hearing Dogs for Deaf People.

A hearing dog seeks out his owner when he hears a sound, such as the telephone or a crying baby. Hearing Dogs for Deaf People teaches dogs to either gently touch their owner with a paw or jump on the owner's lap to communicate that they heard a sound. When a hearing dog is asked "What is it?" either vocally or by sign language, the dog leads his owner to the sound's source. If the sound is a fire or smoke alarm, the dog immediately lies down to indicate danger rather than leading the owner back to the sound.

Although many dogs around the world are trained for this sort of work, Barnaby is unique. For while Barnaby is Marjorie's "ears," she serves as his "eyes"—Barnaby is blind.

Although Barnaby has always been devoted to his work and to Marjorie, the bond between them has grown even stronger since the Golden developed cataracts nearly two years ago. Although many humans faced with such a physical challenge would cut back on their workload or quit entirely, retiring never seems to have crossed Barnaby's mind. Like so many other hearing dogs, he loves his job.

"To him, it's all a game," says Marjorie. "It starts the moment the alarm clock goes off, and he wakes me up. The vet can't see any problem with him continuing to alert me. With a dog like Barnaby, I don't think I could stop him from working even if I tried. He takes pride in his work. I would go so far as to say he works even better with his loss of sight, as if he wants to prove a point. Barnaby is happiest when he's working."

Marjorie and Barnaby are inseparable. Deafness is an invisible disability that can be very isolating. Barnaby helps Marjorie break out of that isolation.

"I now wonder how I coped without a hearing dog," says Marjorie. "I was certainly a lot more introverted. Since I got Barnaby, I have a lot more confidence, which I get from him. He is the best thing that ever happened to me. He alerts me to sounds, makes me aware of things going on around me, and is an icebreaker in any awkward moment."

IVAN

Susan Tucker of Paso Robles, California, first met Ivan in 1991 when she contacted a Kerry Blue Terrier Rescue organization to ask about adopting a puppy. A family had bought Ivan when he was three months old, only to turn him in to a local animal shelter shortly afterward.

The woman who had rescued Ivan from the pound told Susan that he had been in terrible shape when she had picked him up, but with lots of love he had improved tremendously. All Susan saw was a beautiful puppy who was full of life. She immediately offered to take home this "man of her dreams."

The first few days Ivan was in his new home, Susan noticed he followed her closely, often bumping into her leg with his nose. He also kept walking into furniture and other objects around the house. When Susan took him to the veterinarian, she was devastated to learn what was causing his lack of coordination; he had been beaten over the head, and the swelling in his brain was so severe it affected his vision.

Susan was determined to help her newfound friend. She worked closely with her vet and eventually Ivan's swelling was reduced. Ivan was soon able to see with all but his peripheral vision.

Despite the abuse he had endured, Ivan loved everyone, from the assorted people he met on walks to the various animals he encountered; even the bunnies that most terriers would see as prey. Susan took him everywhere she went, from the video store to the thrift store. Ivan was even welcome in many places that normally do not allow dogs. The owner of one shop with a "no dog" policy told Susan that Ivan was better behaved than many of the children who visited the store and that he was welcome any time.

Susan had lived with dogs all her life. In the past, she had learned how to train assistance dogs for the disabled, but she never thought that she might have to train a dog to assist herself. In 1995, Susan found herself on disability for back and neck problems, as well as severe depression, anxiety attacks, and agoraphobia. She wanted to return to school, but she was under strict orders from her doctor not to carry books, a backpack, or pull a cart of books. She turned to Ivan to help her fulfill her dream.

Ivan was a quick learner, and he was already comfortable performing many tasks from his excursions around town with Susan. When Susan first outfitted him with a canine backpack, he sniffed it as if to say, "Is that all?" then trotted off with a spring in his step.

Ivan became increasingly sensitive to changes in Susan's health and did his best to accommodate them. Many times, Ivan was the only encouragement that allowed Susan to leave the house. The day she was to sign up for classes, she was struck with an attack of agoraphobia. She grabbed Ivan and ran to the car, where she hugged him tightly to her chest until her heart stopped pounding. Once she calmed down, she continued to school.

Many days, leaving the house was only the beginning of Susan's challenges. She often would experience anxiety attacks and need to hide in the car or some other quiet place until she felt capable of going on with her day. Sometimes the panic would grip her so tightly that she needed the terrier's help just to reach the car. During these occasions, Ivan sensed Susan's distress and held her attention with his steady gaze or by touching her hand with his reassuring muzzle until they reached the safety of the car. There, Ivan would curl up with Susan, warming her with his furry body and licking dry her tears until she was able to return to class. Although Susan missed many classes and often went home early due to these attacks, she finished the semester with two Bs and a C, thanks to the steadfast assurance of her canine companion.

Sadly, Ivan died just short of his eighth birthday. Fearing that she would never have the strength to leave the house on her own, Susan adopted a three-month-old Standard Poodle to train as her new helpmate. Although Lance is the perfect example of a service dog and large enough to pull the wheelchair that Susan now requires, he will never quite replace Ivan in Susan's heart.

"I have what are called hidden disabilities," says Susan. "You can't see my back and neck problems, arthritis, nerve damage, agoraphobia, anxiety, and chronic depression, but you could see the wonderful dog that helped me face those difficulties. You might have seen me taking a walk with my dog, and I looked perfectly normal. Only I knew that it was the special relationship with my dog that allowed me to walk down that street."

MACGRIFF

Justin Seaver was born in 1981 with Down's Syndrome. He has multiple disabilities due to a stroke he suffered during cardiac surgery, including chronic daily seizures and chronic respiratory problems. He also suffers from severe arthritic hips after two failed hip operations. These disabilities were difficult when he was a child, but they became increasingly harder to deal with as he grew older.

But when Golden Retriever MacGriff arrived in the Seaver home in August 2001 to be Justin's service dog, Justin's parents noticed an immediate, miraculous change in their son.

"Mac and Justin are constant companions and best friends. They go everywhere together," says Cynthia Seaver, Justin's mother.

Mac helps Justin in many ways, from picking up something he's dropped to providing companionship. Mac quickly adjusted to Justin's immobility. He lies on the floor with him, keeping him company for hours. He brings Justin his shoes in the morning and brings balls and toys to Justin, nudging him impatiently until the young man takes the toy and throws it.

Justin's seizures are often severe, but while he used to suffer alone, he now has Mac to provide comfort when he is in pain. When a seizure hits, Mac lies next to Justin and shares his strength until it passes. One day, when Justin experienced a particularly bad seizure, Mac instinctively knew what to do. He ran into the bedroom to get Justin's favorite toy and brought it to the young man without any command. He determined on his own what would best comfort his companion.

Justin suffers with very bad pain from his arthritic hips. Mac gladly allows Justin's parents to position the young man's legs on his back to lessen the pressure on Justin's hips. Mac remains still, waiting patiently until Justin is ready to try another position.

Mac is also a source of strength for Justin during his frequent doctor appointments. Justin often has to endure unpleasant tests and procedures, but Mac is always with him to help him through. Mac lies next to Justin or puts his front paws in Justin's lap and snuggles until Justin feels better.

Now that Justin has Mac, he no longer is afraid to go out in public. Whereas people used to ignore Justin when they encountered him in a store or on the street, they now stop and talk to him about his wonderful dog. "Justin wants to be liked and accepted just like everyone else, and Mac makes that possible," says Cynthia.

Perhaps one of the greatest gifts that Mac has given Justin is a new sense of self-esteem. Justin used to rely on others to take care of him, but now he is responsible for someone else. Justin feeds Mac twice a day and grooms him daily.

"Justin plays catch and tug of war with Mac every chance he gets," says Cynthia. "They sleep together and even get in trouble together! Justin has responsibility for his new friend, and, as a result, he grows more and more with each passing day. Justin has every reason to be proud of the good care he gives his dog. This self-esteem is something he has never felt before. He knows Mac is dependent on him, and he depends on Mac."

Cynthia says bringing Mac and Justin together was a community effort. "We are deeply grateful to the family who raised Mac as a puppy, the trainers at Children's Village, Saxon Middle School—which raised a scholarship for Justin and Mac's training—and the East Coast Assistance Dogs for People With Disabilities for making Mac-Griff possible for our son. These magnificent dogs are a gift from God, and they can do what they do through the help of such committed people."

OPIE

Jody Nibbe of Madison, Wisconsin, has lived with bipolar disorder for twenty-seven years; since she was eleven years old. She admits that for fifteen of those years, she was very destructive. She had an increasingly difficult time managing her illness as she grew older and tried to forge adult relationships. Knowing that her human relationships were suffering, she always found herself gravitating to the animals in her life.

"I've had dogs, cats, rabbits, and horses," says Jody. "A lot of people who suffer from mental illness end up self-medicating with alcohol or drugs. I self-medicated with my animals."

When Jody married and had children, her struggle to maintain mental balance in her life intensified. Adding to her unhappiness was an unsupportive husband who was not an animal person and who tried to convince Jody to give up her pets.

"I felt guilty for needing animals to help me with my illness," Jody says. "For years I just barely survived and my soul began to die."

Then one day, Jody saw a television show about service dogs and how they helped people with disabilities. She spent the next week on her computer searching for information about service dogs and the organizations that train them. She felt in her heart that this was a way she could help others.

Jody found a service dog organization in her city and began attending their classes. After about six weeks, the organization accepted Jody to train dogs for them. "I was ecstatic!" says Jody. "I could actually have a dog at my side twenty-four hours a day. Within just a few short months, I noticed a very drastic change in my ability to manage my own mental illness."

Jody continued to train mobility assistance dogs for the next two years. During that time, she lost both of her own dogs to old age. One of those dogs was a German

Shepherd mix whom Jody had rescued and who had seen Jody through many turbulent times. Shortly after the dog's death, Jody placed the service dog she had been training and found herself without a dog for the first time in her life. At the same time, she quit training with the service organization due to a difference in philosophy. She floundered, knowing she wanted to continue training service dogs, but not sure where to turn. While researching other organizations, she found information on Psychiatric Service Dogs and joined several PSD e-mail support groups to learn more.

That's when Opie found her. She was searching the Internet for rescue dogs who needed a home and came across a description of a three-month-old Australian Shepherd/Blue Heeler mix in Nashville, Tennessee. A shelter volunteer recognized the dog's exceptional personality and temporarily adopted him so he wouldn't be euthanized. Jody wrote to the woman and told her she was looking for a very special dog to work as a service canine. The woman sent Opie's picture, and as soon as she looked at it, Jody knew that he was meant to be hers.

Through the help of rescue volunteers known as the Canine Underground Railroad, Opie was transported from Nashville to Wisconsin by seven volunteer drivers, arriving at Jody's home one April evening. By the following September, Jody's illness was spinning out of control due to a built-up tolerance to her medication. Faced with the prospect of new medication that might or might not work, Jody decided it was time to see if Opie could truly make a difference in her life. She began training him to respond to her manic depression and anxiety episodes; teaching him to stay by her side until the episodes passed. By stroking his fur, staring into his eyes, and snuggling up next to him, Jody was able to stay grounded.

"This is one of the most basic functions that a psychiatric service dog can provide—helping his partner stay grounded in the here and now," Jody explains. "Depression is rooted in events of the past, anxiety is rooted in the fear of the future, and dissociative episodes are a result of the brain locking into a moment of trauma. Grounding exercises help relieve the symptoms of all of these states of mind. Opie responds to all the states and pulls me out so I can continue to function as normally as possible."

Before she had Opie, these episodes were often very destructive for Jody. She would follow whichever path her irrational mind took her, often not even remembering what had happened later. After such an episode, she would spend all her time repairing the damage she had done before the next episode hit. Her life devolved into cycles of destruction and damage control. Opie allows Jody to ride through these episodes without resorting to destructive actions.

Opie is with Jody everywhere she goes. He lies at her feet during the day to make sure she's okay. Jody used to be afraid to leave the house or spend time with family and friends because of her illness. Opie allows her the freedom to have positive, healthy relationships without fearing what havoc her illness might cause next. Opie has also helped Jody to be independent. Whereas she used to feel like a burden for having to lean on family and friends during times when she was non-functional, now she and Opie face each challenge together. This freedom has significantly reduced the number of episodes Jody experiences.

"I haven't had this much fun since childhood, before I was struck with bipolar," says Jody. "Thanks to Opie, my dark days are over and I'm looking forward to 'living' again."

CHAPTER 2

DOGS AS THERAPISTS

Dogs' natural capacity for compassion has been harnessed for a philanthropic endeavor called pet-assisted therapy. Therapy dogs and their owners visit hospitals, nursing homes, psychiatric wards, and children's homes, helping in all types of therapy, from speech therapy to mobility assistance. Although therapy dogs receive training to prepare them for an unfamiliar world of wheelchairs, IV bags, and hospital machinery, no one can teach them the compassion they bring to their volunteer work.

Therapy work can be as simple as a weekly visit to a nursing home to receive pats and kisses from the elderly and the lonely. Or, it can involve much more, such as helping a child recovering from a car accident relearn how to move her arms and hands by grooming a therapy dog.

If you are interested in pursuing therapy work with your dog, contact Delta Society, Therapy Dogs International, or a local therapy group to find out how to get certified. You'll be glad you did—and so will your dog.

MOSS

Val Maurer of Hartville, Ohio, entered the world of therapy dogs before these pets were even labeled therapy animals; a time before Delta Society and other organizations had developed organized programs for visiting hospitals, nursing homes, and psychiatric wards. Val was asked to help train Alex, a dog who was living at a group home for disabled adults. Although Alex was loved by most of the patients, some of the employees considered him to be an unwanted additional responsibility. At the time, caregivers were not as aware as they are today of the positive emotional impact of dogs.

Although Val succeeded in molding Alex into a gentle, mannerly canine, the employees got their way and banned Alex from living at the home. He stayed with Val until she could find a permanent home for him. While Alex was staying with Val, the residents called her and asked if she would bring Alex back for a visit. The administration agreed, and Val embarked on what would become almost two decades of unexpected adventures.

As Val prepared for their first visit, she decided, on a whim, to bring her own dog, a young Border Collie, as well. "I hadn't planned on bringing my Moss along," says Val. "He was such a born rabble-rouser! I got him when he was three months old, and he should have been clingy and impressionable. Instead, he made it clear that he had a mind of his own, and I was just along for the ride."

Val knew that bringing Moss would probably get her in trouble with the caregivers who already disliked dogs, but she was upset with them for not taking Alex back. She thought that by seeing mannerly Alex next to her ten-month-old hellion, they would recognize their mistake. She thought they might learn to appreciate Alex and possibly decide to take him back. She also figured it couldn't hurt to give Moss some socialization, although he probably would behave so horribly they would never be invited back again. On some level, Val almost wished this would happen. Although she derived a lot of satisfaction from visiting at the home, it was very difficult for her emotionally. Here would be her excuse to step back.

Just as Val expected, Moss acted up at every turn. He investigated everything and everybody, zooming into forbidden territory, such as the kitchen and offices. Val found herself constantly yelling at him as he lifted his leg to mark everything as "his" territory. He also proved to be much too pushy for some of the residents, and he outright scared others.

"With his mostly black coat and the intense 'eye' that holds sheep so well but can peer through a person's skull, Moss frightened most people. After encountering Moss, they often said they felt like they were being judged by a wolf."

Things were going so badly that Val knew they wouldn't be asked back. But then something happened that changed everything.

Christine* was a resident with multiple birth defects who sat in a large, custom-built wheelchair. She was deaf, and her language consisted only of emotional tonalities.

* Name has been changed for privacy.

Often her emotions would escape from her lips in a screech. She was paraplegic, very small and stocky, with short black hair that hung over dark eyes that brooded over the world that moved beyond her. Christine was afraid of dogs, and she reacted with violent screams and gestures if any dog came near her.

Val kept Moss and Alex far from Christine to avoid upsetting her. But after a while, Christine began screaming excitedly. Everyone thought that the dogs were too close to her, so Val got up and looked at her to see how far away she wanted the dogs to be. Christine rapidly signed to her fellow residents and the employees that she wanted Moss to come to her.

Val couldn't believe it! Moss? Of all the dogs she had seen in the home, Christine wanted to play with him? Here was a dog whose looks scared most people and whose lack of manners frustrated and embarrassed his owner. And tiny, fragile Christine, who was terrified of the cutest Spaniels and Toy Poodles wanted to play with Moss. For some inexplicable reason, these two not only fell in love with each other immediately, but they also both behaved better with each other than they did with anyone else. Val knew she was now doomed to somehow make her visits work.

The challenge was to find a way for Christine to play with Moss in a manner that they could both understand. Val decided to try to teach Moss some basic sign language. First, she taught him that one handclap meant, "Come." Then she taught him hand signals for "Give me the ball," "Catch the ball," "Sit," and "Good." Two weeks later they returned to the home and an aide explained to Christine how to communicate with Moss.

Her dark eyes danced with excitement and the two of them happily played catch for hours while Val, the caregivers, and the rest of the residents watched in disbelief.

The dog Val knew as an obnoxious, frustrating puppy who had failed every obedience class in a tricounty area was suddenly a perfectly behaved Border Collie, patiently catching and retrieving an erratically thrown tennis ball that bounced haphazardly around the room. For her part, Christine, whom Val had only seen throwing violent temper tantrums, now received the tennis ball from Moss with trembling, but calm hands. On that day and during all their future visits, when Christine and Moss got together, Val only saw two gentle souls helping each other.

Eventually, Christine's health deteriorated, and she spent more time in bed. It became a struggle for Moss to visit with Christine because animals were not allowed anywhere other than in the common room and the outer hallway. Even the few aides who were dog lovers and recognized the difference Moss had made in Christine's life were not able to smuggle him into Christine's room. Sadly, Christine wasn't able to experience Moss's loving compassion even one more time before her death.

Still, Moss continued to visit the residence. He began to mature and to think of needs and interests outside of his own. He found other people who needed him. Somehow, this pup who hated to be cuddled, figured out that another resident, Anne, needed to express love physically. Although the home's rules forbade visitors to touch or be touched by the residents due to health reasons, the aides made an exception for Moss. They would move Anne from her wheelchair into a recliner. Moss climbed into her

RAINBOW BRIDGE

Just this side of Heaven is a place called Rainbow Bridge. When an animal dies who has been especially close to someone here, that pet goes to Rainbow Bridge. There are meadows and hills for all our special friends so they can run and play together. There is plenty of food, water, and sunshine, and our friends are warm and comfortable. All the animals who had been ill or old are restored to health and vigor; those who were hurt or maimed are made whole and strong again, just as we remember them in our dreams of days gone by. The animals are happy and content, except for one small thing; they each miss someone very special to them who had to be left behind.

They all run and play together, but the day comes when one suddenly stops and looks into the distance. His bright eyes are intent; his eager body quivers. Suddenly he begins to run from the group, flying over the green grass, his legs carrying him faster and faster. You have been spotted, and when you and your special friend finally meet, you cling to each other in joyous reunion, never to be parted again. The happy kisses rain upon your face, your hands again caress the beloved head, and you look once more into the trusting eyes of your pet, so long gone from your life but never absent from your heart.

Then you cross the Rainbow Bridge together.

—Author unknown
(www.rainbowbridge.tierranet.com/bridge.htm)

---

lap, and the two exchanged hugs and kisses until Anne was exhausted with laughter.

Moss also discovered that another resident of the home, Glen, needed to get away from the constant companionship of people. Glen would take walks alone with just Moss as his silent companion. The two looked as if they were going off on a quiet hike through the woods even though they were actually walking up and down the home's long hallway. Although Moss had always refused to heel at Val's side during obedience classes, instead dragging her around every time she put on his leash, with Glen, who lurched as he walked, Moss walked on leash as if he were the top obedience dog in the country.

"Our original, unintended compassion toward Christine taught both of us that we could be much more than we ever imagined," says Val. Eventually, however, due to the stress of juggling the residents' needs, dealing with the aides who didn't want Moss at the home, and Val's developing health problems, she and Moss stopped their visits.

Still, Val didn't want to lose the incredible partnership she had forged with Moss. She decided to take the therapy skills they had learned through their work with the people in the residency and apply it to teaching Border Collies who are rescued from abandonment how to live with hope and trust and to learn basic manners.

"We eventually saved hundreds of Border Collies and Border Collie mixes," says Val. "We finally retired when Moss got too old and arthritic to want to do anything more than lay at my side, and I finally had to say good-bye.

"I hope one of the first things he did when he crossed that Rainbow Bridge was go find Christine and play a gentle game of catch with her."

SADIE

Owners who embark on therapy work with their dogs are rarely prepared for the emotional impact their visits will have on themselves, their dogs, and the patients they meet. Joe Gangloff and his Golden Retriever, Sadie, routinely visit medical centers, psychiatric units, churches, and assisted living centers in North Carolina. Joe and Sadie have witnessed many tears on their visits, but have also been able to bring laughter and joy to people who need it most.

Sadie and Joe usually don't visit anyone more than once because the units they visit are designed to treat patients and discharge them as soon as possible. Many patients, however, delay their discharge from the morning to the late afternoon on the days that they know Sadie is scheduled for a visit so they can see her a second time before returning home.

One day, Sadie and Joe visited a charming elderly woman whom they had met on a previous visit to the restorative care unit. When they entered her room, Joe asked how she was doing. The woman replied that the past two weeks had been difficult. She was re-admitted shortly after being discharged, and doctors amputated her right leg below the knee. Despite this tragedy, a smile creased the woman's face when she saw Sadie. She assured Joe, "It's okay, because I get to see Sadie again." She then asked to have a picture taken with Sadie that she could keep by her bedside.

While Sadie's visits are meant to help the patients, Joe discovered that pet therapy often helps the staff as well. Each time Joe and Sadie enter a hospital environment, they encounter patients, visitors, physicians, and other staff members who show anxiety through their facial expressions and body language. Regardless of their purpose for being at the hospital, once these people spot Sadie and ask to pet her, their demeanor instantly changes.

Joe says, "In all of our visits, no one has ever left an encounter with Sadie without a broad smile on their face and a newly found spring in their step." One physician even requested that she be interrupted whenever Sadie enters the unit so that she can start her day with her own pet therapy. When she gets the call that Sadie has arrived, she stops whatever she is doing, whether she is by herself, with a patient, or even in a meeting with patients, family members, and medical students. A few moments with the Golden Retriever are enough to rejuvenate her and allow her to face any challenges the day may present.

Sadie even helped one nurse overcome her fear of dogs. The woman showed only mild interest in Sadie when they first met, and she revealed that she had been bitten as a child. Therefore, she kept her distance from the Golden. After encountering Sadie on several visits, however, the nurse worked up the courage to talk to the dog and then to pet her. Joe assured the woman that if she wanted to get over her fear of dogs, Sadie was the perfect animal to help because of her loving, gentle nature. Eventually, the nurse began to look forward to Sadie's visits and finally trusted Sadie enough to give her big bear hugs, which Sadie responded to with wriggling delight. From that day on, whenever the nurse saw Sadie, she proudly announced to anyone nearby that she used to be afraid of dogs, but Sadie helped her overcome her fear.

Sometimes visits with Sadie resulted in humorous occasions. One morning, for example, Joe and Sadie were assisting an elderly woman who was learning how to use a walker as part of her recovery from hip surgery. A therapist walked to the patient's right to provide any assistance she might need. Joe walked to the left of the patient to control Sadie's movements if necessary, and Sadie walked between Joe and the patient with her leash under the patient's hand on the bar of the walker. Sadie slowly ambled alongside the patient, frequently glancing up to adjust her pace. As they made their way down the hall, they passed the patient's hospital roommate who was undergoing a different type of therapy. The trio burst into laughter as they heard the roommate remark to her therapist, "I didn't know Mrs. Jones was blind!" Joe says that was the first time, but not the last, that Sadie was mistaken for a guide dog!

DUSTY

Sometimes dogs open up whole new worlds to their owners. If it weren't for a special Collie named Dusty, Gail Kalina of Glenview, Illinois, would never have discovered the rewards of therapy work.

Gail first started obedience training Dusty when he was about a year old. Dusty turned out to be a challenging student, whining from stress during the entire twelve weeks of their first class.

"He was certainly the most easily distracted and silliest Collie you'd ever met," muses Gail. But the instructor, Kathy McCarthy, convinced Gail to continue with Dusty's training. After about six months, Kathy approached Gail after class and asked her if she would be interested in doing therapy with Dusty.

"I had no idea what she was talking about," recalls Gail. "I asked, 'Is Dusty really so bad that he needs therapy?'" Kathy laughed and explained that she and several other friends were thinking about starting a therapy dog group to work with special-needs children. Over the past six months, Dusty's gentle nature and obvious love of the children who came to training classes with their parents had impressed Kathy. She recalled the time a little boy was playing next to Dusty and used the Collie's long nose as a landing strip for his toy helicopter. Kathy thought Dusty would be a natural at therapy work, and children would love to pet his long, beautiful coat.

Gail agreed to give therapy work a try. She had recently gone through a divorce and thought this might be a way to put her own life back together while she was helping others. A week later, Gail joined Kathy and her friends, and they formed Rainbow Therapy Dogs, named after their training room at the YMCA, which had large rainbows painted along one wall.

"We were reminded of the saying: 'To reach a rainbow, one must reach high,'" says Gail. "We thought that was appropriate for our goals."

At first, the group's visitations were meant to entertain the children. They would demonstrate obedience routines, perform some tricks, and let the children pet the dogs. After their third visit to a school, they noticed that the children were trying to emulate their commands. One of the teachers, who was a member of Rainbow Therapy Dogs, convinced the school's director to let the group come to the school on a regular basis to try to teach the children how to handle the dogs.

"It was unbelievable how the children responded," says Gail. "The dogs were able to break through to children who wouldn't let adults reach them."

For the next eight years, Gail and Dusty filled their days helping others. Gail fondly remembers a boy they often visited at a residential facility on Saturday mornings. "One little boy was brought into the day room and placed next to Dusty. We held the boy's hands and helped him pet Dusty's long, silky fur. The little boy relaxed and leaned forward to rub his face in Dusty's fur. After a while, we noticed the little boy had fallen asleep with his head on Dusty's chest. Dusty had also fallen asleep and together they lay there, breathing in harmony. Dusty didn't move until our session was finished about twenty minutes later. After that, when Dusty went to work there, he knew to lie down by the window and wait for 'his' little boy."

Gail also recalls how Dusty would position himself between the children and the door whenever he heard a loud noise or voice in the hallway outside the room. She believes this was the Collie's way of protecting his "flock" of children.

Gail says her most moving experience occurred at a rehabilitation center. A nurse asked her to take a moment to visit with a fifteen-year-old young man who was lying on a gurney. He had been shot in the back and was being a very difficult patient.

Gail sat Dusty on the chair next to the gurney, and the Collie put his paw on the teenager's arm. When Gail asked the boy if he would like to pet Dusty, he refused to respond and continued staring blankly at the wall. After two more attempts to get him to communicate, Gail said to Dusty, "This boy needs a kiss. Dusty, please give him lots of kisses."

The boy turned his head away, refusing to look at Dusty. Gail responded, "Listen hear, I just drove over an hour in rush-hour traffic to visit you, and you're going to pet my dog." She picked Dusty up and laid him across the boy so Dusty could give him a kiss. "Dusty looked at the young man with his famous bewildered Collie expression," says Gail. "A few seconds passed and then the boy's arms came up around Dusty and he hugged Dusty, buried his face in Dusty's chest, and started sobbing. The young man's nurse and mother, who were standing off to the side, started crying, too. It was the first time this boy had showed any emotion. I guess he wasn't the tough gangbanger he pretended to be. His mom and nurse thanked me over and over again for not giving up.

"Many years later, just before Dusty left us and crossed that Rainbow Bridge, our vet was looking at Dusty's chest x-ray, and he mentioned that Dusty's heart was somewhat smaller than he expected. I said, 'No, Dr. Jeff, Dusty has the biggest heart in the whole world.'"

JAKE

Golden Retrievers are known for their love of children. A special Golden named Jake has taken that emotion one step further by giving unconditional love and support to children facing the frightening uncertainties and pain of terminal illness.

Danielle Wilson of Hurdle Mills, North Carolina, says six-and-a-half-year-old Jake "leaves his paw prints on the hearts of every person he meets." Jake has been registered as a therapy dog with Therapy Dogs International since his first birthday. He has received numerous awards for his service, including the Golden Retriever

Club of America's first ever Gold Standard Award for "Inspiring and Enriching People for a Lifetime" and the 2001 American Kennel Club's Award for Canine Excellence (ACE) in the Therapy Dog category.

Having also earned ten titles in agility and obedience, Jake is a well-rounded canine. Although Jake enjoys these competitive sports, however, he seems to prefer therapy work to all other activities.

Jake frequently visits Duke Medical Center as a Delta Pet Partner and has served as mentor for several dogs in the volunteer program as they earned their Delta Pet Partner certification. In 2001, Danielle and Jake helped Duke raise more than $891,000 by participating in the medical center's annual radio-a-thon. Danielle says Jake was so popular that callers wanted to talk to him before they sent in their pledge.

Jake and three other Pet Partner Teams also visit the Ronald McDonald House in Durham, North Carolina, every month to provide a positive distraction for children suffering from serious illnesses. Although Jake makes friends wherever he goes, he has forged the deepest bonds with the children he met as a member of Duke Children's Hospital's Critical Care Unit Pet Therapy Program. He often wears a fire hat on these visits and cuddles in bed with children who are immobile. He loves to ham it up and perform tricks, and is often called a ray of "Golden Sunshine" in the sterile hospital environment. Many children who are totally unresponsive to human interaction light up, become vocal, and respond only to Jake.

During five years of volunteer work at Duke, Jake formed a special bond with one eight-year-old boy named

Brad.* Danielle later found out that Brad's sole motivation for coming to Duke to receive his chemotherapy treatments was that Jake was always there for Pet Therapy visits. After learning this, Danielle scheduled their visits to coincide with Brad's appointments so Jake could sit with the boy as he received his treatments. Danielle and Jake got to know Brad's family during the nine months of his illness. When the cancer reached Brad's brain and it appeared the little boy's battle was coming to an end, the hospital requested that Danielle and Jake come to provide comfort to the family during his final week. Jake cuddled on the bed in the Pediatric Intensive Care Unit and seemed to understand the sadness around him. Danielle says, "We were there the night another angel got his wings." Jake and Danielle were invited to the funeral and have remained close with Brad's family.

In January 1998, Danielle was devastated when she discovered a lump on Jake's side that was found to be cancerous. Danielle wondered how a dog, whose purpose in life was to provide comfort to terminally ill children, could be terminally ill himself. She opted to have the tumor removed to prevent the cancer from spreading. Jake's beautiful fur was shaved bald and three layers of muscle were removed. Despite a long rehabilitation, Jake continued to visit Duke. He became a source of inspiration and a connection for children who had cancer and who had lost their hair due to chemotherapy. Jake's win over this devastating disease also gave many children hope that they too would be victorious in their own battles.

* Name has been changed for privacy.

In addition to visiting hospitals, Jake often accompanies Danielle to the school where she works. He helps her present a Prevent-a-Bite program to grades K–5, which teaches children how to avoid getting bitten by dogs. Danielle also uses Jake to motivate children to read. Several times a month, Jake visits the school library for a "Golden-Read-In," during which he "reads" with children who have met their reading goals. Since incorporating Jake into the program, Danielle has noticed a substantial difference in the students' reading habits. Jake's positive effect on children has inspired Danielle to pursue a master's degree in school guidance counseling.

Danielle says, "With Animal Assisted Therapy, I can integrate a dog's healing touch and reach the difficult children society has forgotten. This is my mission, and I have Jake to thank for the inspiration."

Danielle knew Jake was a hero to the children he has helped, but one day his heroic nature was called into action closer to home. Danielle's husband, Doug, suddenly began having seizures several years after being hit by a drunk driver. When Doug had his second seizure, Jake leaped into the armchair where Doug was sitting and laid across his master, pinning him down and licking his face until the seizure ended. Danielle was amazed—Jake never received seizure alert or service dog training, but instinctively knew he needed to keep Doug still to prevent him from falling and getting hurt.

Danielle says, "The experience reconfirmed the uniqueness of this beloved dog."

ADAM

Many people who have near-death experiences report phenomenal changes in their lives. Most say that they discover a new meaning to life and want to share that new meaning with others. Some are moved to switch careers, finding a new vocation in which they can help those in need. But what about animals? After facing death and surviving, do animals also experience a newfound love of life and wish to share that love with others? The story of Adam seems to suggest this is true.

Suzanne Sims met Adam on March 2, 1993, when the year-old dog was brought into the Mississippi Animal Rescue League where Suzanne worked. Suzanne remembers her first sight of him: The doors to the shelter opened, and a man walked in carrying a gorgeous tricolored dog weighing about 45 to 50 pounds. When the man put the dog down, the terrified animal dropped flat to the floor, urinating everywhere. His eyes were huge and filled with fear. Suzanne went to the dog immediately to try to reassure him. She thought he was either a Border Collie or Border Collie/Australian Shepherd mix, but she couldn't tell for sure. All she knew was that this dog had suffered a great deal of abuse. Later, she would discover the terrified dog was a purebred Australian Shepherd.

The dog's story broke her heart. The man who brought him in was a property owner. His tenants had moved out of state, and when he went to check the property, he found two dogs. This dog was the lucky one—the other dog didn't survive.

Suzanne sensed something special in the Aussie. She knew he would be held for five days as a stray to give his owner time to claim him, and then he would probably be put to sleep due to his fear and lack of trust. Still, every day after she finished her duties at the shelter, she took him out of his kennel and into the office, where they sat on the floor and got to know each other. By the end of the five days, the Aussie was jumping up on the kennel door when he saw Suzanne. The shelter's technician told Suzanne she had planned to euthanize him, but changed her mind when she saw how much progress he made in five short days. She officially listed him for adoption.

Suzanne continued to work with the Aussie, and even began to call him Adam, a name she never would have chosen had she planned on adopting him, but it came to her one day and seemed to fit him. Suzanne held her breath every time someone seemed interested in him and added him to her prayers every night. She would be devastated if he was euthanized after all he had overcome. As much as she wanted to adopt Adam herself, she was living in small quarters with her two dogs, Sissy and Bouvier, so she didn't have room for another dog.

Finally, one day a woman visiting the shelter with her two daughters put back a puppy they had been looking at to adopt Adam. Since puppies were rarely passed over for older dogs, Suzanne was sure this was the right home for Adam. Adam stayed at the shelter to be neutered, and Suzanne checked on him every hour. Adam came through the surgery fine, but a few days later the woman called to say she couldn't take Adam. Her daughters had brought home a puppy while they were waiting for Adam, and the puppy died. The woman realized that their last two dogs had died in the same manner and wondered if there was a danger at their house that needed to be cleared up before they brought home another dog. Suzanne was glad for the woman's concern for

Adam's well-being, but she was worried that he might not get another chance at adoption.

Thankfully, Suzanne's prayers were answered, and a couple adopted Adam shortly afterward. Once again, however, Adam was returned. He had tested positive for heartworms, and the couple wasn't able to see him through the time-consuming course of treatment. As Suzanne wrote an in-ticket for Adam, she choked back tears, unable to speak. She knew this was probably the end for him. Heartworms are a death sentence at a shelter where many healthy animals are euthanized.

Desperate for a way to save Adam, Suzanne called her veterinarian to ask what he would charge to treat a dog Adam's size. When the vet quoted $175, her heart sank; as a grad student working at an animal shelter, she simply couldn't afford it. A coworker at the shelter who knew how Suzanne felt about Adam gave her the name and number of another vet. The tech there, who used to work at the shelter, said they could treat Adam for $75. Suzanne's boyfriend paid for the treatment, and she set to work saving Adam's life.

For four weeks after the first series of medication, Adam had to be kept completely crated except to eat and relieve himself. This would be difficult for any dog, but was especially so for the high-energy Australian Shepherd. Adam stayed in the surgery area of the shelter during the week and went home with Suzanne on weekends, where he became instant best friends with Sissy, Suzanne's Soft-Coated Wheaten Terrier mix. After a second series of medication and a final heartworm test, Adam was found to be clear of the disease.

Once more, Adam was placed for adoption, this time heartworm-free, basic obedience trained, and housebroken. Potential owner after potential owner stopped by his cage, but none made the commitment to take him home. During the four months that had passed since Adam first came into the shelter, Suzanne had become increasingly attached to him. Although it had been impossible for Suzanne to adopt Adam when she first met him, during Adam's recovery she had found a large house with a 6,000-square-foot fenced yard. Suzanne's prayers were answered, and Adam came home to live with her. The day Suzanne signed the adoption papers, five people asked about Adam, and one man begged to adopt him. Suzanne politely refused—she knew Adam belonged with her.

Adam quickly showed aptitude in obedience, tracking, and agility, but there was one area in which Adam truly shined—therapy work. Perhaps Adam's numerous brushes with death made him particularly sensitive to the pain and sadness in others.

"Adam really seems to be able to communicate with these patients, especially those who are not able to speak," says Suzanne. "He seems to sense what they need, what they want, and what they don't want. Several times he has walked up to brain injury patients who had not been able to control their saliva or express any emotions. These people picked up their arms to pet Adam, which was the first movement of any kind for these patients since their injury."

Suzanne says each visit is remarkable in its own way, but some stand out as being truly special. On one visit, a young man was sitting in a wheelchair watching a ball game. The man could not speak, but had regained control of his face muscles, so he could smile. The recreational therapist tried several times to get him to join the group interacting with Suzanne and her dogs, but he refused.

Suzanne was amazed by what Adam did next. While Suzanne and the dogs were visiting the other patients, Adam pulled on his lead to get to the young man. Realizing what he was doing, Suzanne followed. Adam sat down beside the man's chair, put his paw up on the arm of the wheelchair, and touched the young man's arm. He then began watching TV! The man smiled, turned his attention to Adam, and began to pet him.

"Our Bouvier is a huge TV watcher," says Suzanne. "Once, he sat through the entire 'Babe' movie and never moved. But neither of our other dogs ever paid attention to the television before this."

"Adam was so gentle, never insistent, but patient and loving," says Suzanne. "It was an amazing moment."

On another occasion, Suzanne and Adam were visiting a nursing home. As they walked down the hallway, Adam stopped, refusing to move forward. He was shaking and turned around to go back in the opposite direction. Suzanne tried to get him to continue, but he refused, which was something he had never done before. The nurse accompanying them remarked that the room Adam refused to pass was that of a dying patient who probably would not make it through the night.

Adam also showed this amazing sensitivity to death when his best canine friend, Suzanne's Wheaten mix, died just before Christmas 2001. When Sissy died, Suzanne felt she should bring both her other dogs in to see she was gone.

"Adam came in first and was so dignified," says Suzanne. "I think he knew what had happened. He sat down beside me, and I was crying almost uncontrollably. He looked down at Sissy, reached to touch her foot with his nose, and then to my amazement he looked straight up as if he were praying, grieving, or perhaps speaking to Sissy. Then he leaned over to me to give me comfort." For weeks after, Adam climbed on the couch with Suzanne when she was particularly sad and caressed her arm with his paw, as he has done so many times with others in need of comfort.

Perhaps Adam is an innately sensitive dog. Or perhaps, his time spent on death row at the shelter gave him a greater appreciation for life that he now chooses to share with others.

"Adam is a prime example of what tender love, care, and patience can do for any animal, no matter what happened in its past," says Suzanne. "Anyone can hold the key to an animal's future happiness. You must, however, be willing to show them the way."

LUCY

Due to media reports on dog attacks by related breeds, the public has unjustly become wary of all Mastiffs. Dogs like Lucy can do much to teach people the true nature of the breed.

Lucy and her owner, Alison Roby, were volunteers with the San Francisco SPCA's Animal Assisted Therapy program. Although they met many special people during their rounds, one little girl was unforgettable. Katie had leukemia and was not expected to live much longer. The first day Alison and Lucy visited the children's cancer ward at their local hospital, Katie could barely contain her excitement at meeting the huge dog. She immediately patted the bed, calling, "Come on! Come here!" Alison feared Lucy, who weighed in at 170 pounds, might prove too much for the frail little girl. But her concerns were quelled when Lucy gently hopped up onto the bed and rewarded Katie with a kiss.

Katie commented on Lucy's big tongue, then proceeded to recite the weight of a whale's tongue. She continued entertaining Alison with facts she had gleaned in her short life as an animal lover, all the while hugging, kissing, petting, and playing with Lucy until she was exhausted. Alison and Lucy didn't want to overstay their welcome, so they bid farewell to their newfound friend.

A few weeks later, Alison received a call from the director of the therapy program. Katie had been given just a few weeks to live, and the Make-a-Wish Foundation was seeking to grant her wish. And what was her request? Simply to spend more time with Lucy.

Alison and Lucy went back to the hospital for a special visit with Katie that could last as long as she wanted. The first thing Lucy did was bound up onto the bed with Katie. She lay with her head on Katie's stomach, watching with rapt attention as Katie once again stroked the huge Mastiff and shared various facts about the animal kingdom with her visitors. Katie had learned Lucy's two tricks at the last visit—catching anything in her mouth that was tossed into the air and giving a "high five" for treats. Katie proudly showed these tricks to all new visitors to the room.

At one point, Katie felt Lucy must be tired from all this performing. She lifted Lucy's massive head and put a pillow under it to make the dog more comfortable. Katie rested her head next to Lucy's, and they lay on the bed together for hours as people came and went. Lucy seemed to sense that Katie needed her full attention; she didn't react to anyone in the room except the little girl.

Finally, Katie said she was very tired, and although she didn't want them to go, it was time for Alison and Lucy to leave. With a final kiss, Lucy and Katie said their good-byes.

A couple of weeks later, Alison received a call from a nurse at the hospital who was passing on a message from Katie's mother. Alison learned that before Lucy's visit, Katie had been extremely worried about going home for her last few weeks. She was afraid of the potential pain and wasn't sure if she wanted to go home at all. After her time with Lucy, however, she was calm, relaxed, and eager to go home. She told her mother that she knew everything would be fine.

Katie spent her last days with her family. When the time came for her to go, she smiled and said: "I'm going for a walk." Perhaps in that moment, the spirit of a gentle canine giant was accompanying her on her final journey.

TUGGERS AND JEWEL

In cases of severe child abuse or neglect, dogs can often prompt communication from a youngster who has rebuffed all human interaction. Cindy VanNieuwberg of

Fairfield, California, has experienced this amazing connection firsthand during visits with children and teens in a psychiatric hospital accompanied by her two Mastiffs, Tuggers and Jewel, as part of a group called Paws For Healing.

Cindy remembers one girl who had not uttered a word since arriving at the hospital two weeks earlier. After a few minutes of visiting with Tuggers, the girl not only was talking to the massive dog, who was lying with his head in her lap, she was also able to open up to Cindy as well.

Another time, Cindy was briefed about a six-year-old girl whose mother had sold her for sex to obtain drugs. The hospital workers tried everything to get the little girl to interact and respond to others, but no matter what they did, she showed no emotion. When Cindy entered the common room with Jewel, all the other children flocked around the Mastiff, but the little girl stayed separate from the group and remained in her chair. Cindy asked all the children to be seated, then asked the little girl if she wanted Jewel to visit. The girl nodded yes, which was all the encouragement the dog needed. Jewel loped over to the girl, wiggling from head to toe, and showered her with exuberant kisses. A slight smile creased the corners of the little girl's mouth, then she couldn't hold back any longer. She threw her arms around Jewel's neck and hugged the dog tightly. Jewel responded with more wiggles, and the girl finally let out a hearty laugh. Although she had a long road ahead of her and much pain to overcome, this shattered little girl, who had given up all hope, opened herself up to a moment of happiness due to the selfless love of a dog.

MOLLY

On July 2, 1995, tragedy struck Sue and Steve Waite's family when Steve's father, Floyd, suffered a brain aneurysm. He was admitted to the hospital, where all he could do was lie in bed with a breathing tube in his throat. He was able only to wink an eye and occasionally squeeze a family member's hand. Floyd experienced a second aneurysm a couple of weeks later. Floyd's body was fine, but for all the family knew, his brain was no longer functioning. The family tried everything they could think of to get a response from him, but nothing worked. The doctors said it was impossible to know if any of their attempts to communicate were reaching him. They advised the family to continue to talk to him and treat him as if he could hear them, just in case.

The day after Floyd's first attack, the Waite's Rottweiler, Jezzie Belle, gave birth to a litter of puppies. Sue spent the next several weeks running back and forth between home and the hospital, trying to care for her new litter and visit her father-in-law. As the weeks went by, it seemed more unlikely that the family would ever make a connection with Floyd. After a while, he left the hospital and was placed in a nursing home.

Meanwhile, one of the Rottie pups, named Molly, was growing into a particularly sweet, bouncy little girl. When she reached her six-week birthday, Sue decided to take Molly to the nursing home to see Floyd. Sue thought it would be good for the puppy to become socialized to some new people at this stage in her development, and the nursing home's long hallways would be a great opportunity to introduce Molly to a leash. She also thought Floyd might enjoy seeing Molly, although she didn't want to hold out false hope about how he would respond.

Molly was a hit from the moment she walked in the nursing home's front door. She didn't let anyone pass her without greeting them with kisses, all the while wagging her stubby tail so furiously her whole body wriggled. Several nurses stopped to pet her, then asked if she could visit specific patients who were dog lovers. It seemed to take them forever to reach Floyd's room.

When they finally walked in the door, Sue's heart sank. Floyd lay on the bed with his eyes open, staring at nothing. He seemed unaware that they had entered the room. Sue and Steve talked to him, telling him how their day went, who the Cleveland Indians were playing, and how the game went the night before. They kept talking, although they had no idea if he was really hearing any of their conversation.

Sue then decided to put Molly on Floyd's chest. She didn't really believe it would help, but she also didn't think it would do any harm. Molly immediately crawled up to Floyd's face and started kissing him. She worked her way around to his neck, then to his ear. She kept licking Floyd, not caring that he wasn't responding with pats and praise the way most people would. She kissed him as enthusiastically as she had greeted all the people in the hallway who had showered her with attention.

Then it happened; Floyd smiled. Next, he slowly drew his shoulder up to his ear; Molly was tickling him! His smile grew broader and broader, and his eyes widened. Steve and Sue looked at each other in amazement. This was Floyd's first response to anything since his aneurysm. The doctors couldn't get him to show the simplest sign of comprehension, but Molly had gotten him to smile.

Sue decided to test Floyd's response further. She put Molly on his stomach, then picked up his hand and placed it on the plump little Rottie. She told Floyd she had to leave for a minute, and he needed to hold onto Molly to keep her from falling.

The next thing that happened was nothing short of a miracle. Floyd raised his other arm and held Molly tightly with both hands. Sue never had any intention of leaving the bedside, but she could have if she wanted. Floyd had such a strong grip on Molly that the pup wasn't going anywhere.

Sue and Steve were stunned. Molly showed them that although Floyd wasn't able to move well, show emotion, or even move his eyes, he still was there! Sue and Steve choked back their tears as they realized he really had understood all their hours of one-way conversations.

They ended their visit and hurried home to tell the family about their discovery. Everyone wanted to make a date to meet at Floyd's room with Molly to watch his reactions to her.

"These were the last reactions we ever got from Dad, but we were happy the family saw this wonderful man—who made the world laugh—smile one last time," says Sue. "I personally will never be able to repay Molly for what she did that summer. I did however, promise her the best life she could ever imagine, and that she would never leave my home."

In a dog's eyes, that is the best repayment we can give.

MURFEE

Carolyn Uhlin knew that her yellow Labrador Retriever, Murfee, had touched the lives of many during his work as a therapy dog. She didn't understand the true extent of his compassion, however, and what it meant to the thousands of people he met during his lifetime until his death in the fall of 2001.

Murfee entered Carolyn's life when he was released from training as a guide dog at Guiding Eyes for the Blind in New York. Although Murfee excelled in the training program, veterinarians discovered he had hip dysplasia. This degenerative disease of the hip socket prevented him from carrying out the physically demanding work of a guide dog.

Carolyn, who is a psychiatric nurse, got Murfee when he was about a year and a half old. She decided to train this sweet, steadfast dog for therapy work, with the goal of taking him to work with her at the Guilford County Mental Health Center in High Point, North Carolina. Murfee showed natural empathy for the mentally ill patients Carolyn treated. In his spare time, he and his owner also visited nursing homes and schools, sharing unconditional love and a sympathetic ear to countless people. During his nine years as a therapy dog certified by the Delta Society, Murfee became something of a local celebrity. The Guilford County Humane Society presented him with the Animal of the Year Award, and numerous newspaper articles and television spots featured the affable Lab. He was also the first therapy dog in the nation certified by the American Red Cross to comfort disaster victims.

More important than his fame, however, was the personal impact he had on everyone he met. Carolyn recalls the nursing home resident whom, upon meeting Murfee, broke her six-year silence to tell the Lab how beautiful he was. Or the schizophrenic patients who expressed feelings to Murfee that were too painful to discuss with another human being. As beloved by the staff as he was by the patients, Murfee was a valued coworker at The Guilford Center.

Murfee had battled mast cell cancer for three years and was in remission, but his hip dysplasia had worsened. Carolyn knew the end was near. For six months, she tried to prepare the staff and patients at the center for the inevitable. Carolyn cut Murfee's schedule down to half-days until even that became too much for him to handle. The last three weeks of his life, Carolyn cuddled with Murfee and cried, knowing each precious moment was a gift that would soon be gone. When Murfee looked up at her on his last day, his eyes had lost their dignity, and Carolyn knew she had to let Murfee go. She called her supervisor at work and told the woman she would not be in that afternoon because of Murfee's death. She braced herself for the pain and loss her family would endure, but she could never imagine how the community would react to his passing.

The next morning, Carolyn willed herself to get out of bed, determined to get through the first day of work knowing her trusted companion was gone forever. She prepared herself for the memories she would experience as she reached the parking lot, entered the building, and finally faced Murfee's bed, water bowl, and toys lying in the corner of her office. Carolyn knew she would endure pain and tears, but she felt her coworkers would understand.

"What happened when I reached work was a gift," says Carolyn. "I was met with hugs, tears, and sadness from those around me. Their grief was evident. They had lost a coworker and a source of unconditional love that they had come to depend upon over the years. They stepped in to help me when they could and allowed me to retreat to my office and deal with my pain. I received flowers, cards, e-mails, and calls from members of the staff and the administration. Telling the patients was overwhelming, despite the help from the staff. When least expected, small acts of kindness brought tears and smiles. One of the local radio talk show hosts spoke of Murfee's death on his program and talked about the loss for the community and for me."

"The patients were so very compassionate and their feelings gave me such strength," Carolyn continues. "Their smiles would turn to tears as I told them of his death. Many of them thanked me for sharing him with them. They wanted to hug me, give me cards, and tell me how much Murfee meant to them. This scene was repeated many times a day for weeks. The thing that was most difficult, however, was the unexpected wave of emotion that hit when I met with particular patients who had a special bond with Murfee or who had passed a particular milestone with him. It was like standing with my back to the ocean. I never knew when the 'big wave' was going to hit."

Carolyn also discovered an outpouring of support from outside the center. During every trip to the mall, the grocery store, or the drugstore, people who knew Murfee stopped Carolyn and asked how she was and what had caused Murfee's death. Many people made contributions to Guiding Eyes for the Blind in Murfee's memory.

"With the loss of a family pet, the sadness is shared by a few individuals," says Carolyn. "But with Murfee, the loss involved the thousands of people he had met through the years. I received notes from people who had met him more than seven years earlier. Some of the people told me stories that I had not even been aware of about how Murfee had affected their lives. I continued to be amazed by how much Murfee had done and how much a therapy dog can achieve."

"I feel fortunate to have been chosen to give Murfee a purpose in life and help him to reach his full potential." But with his death, Carolyn had realized the impact of the loss and the love that so many people felt for Murfee. Even as she grieved, she had to put her own emotions on hold at times and soothe their sadness. "Yes, it is painful to let go, but the time I spent with him was a joyful journey. To know that he touched so many lives during those years is priceless."

LACEY JANE

Gail Zukow of San Juan Capistrano, California, remembers the first time she met Lacey Jane the Doberman Pinscher: "She had soft brown eyes, long silky ears, a tail like Pluto, and long gangly legs. I thought she looked very strange, as I had always had Dobies with their ears cropped and tails docked. Little did I know the joy and comfort this one-year-old lady would bring to many people."

Lacey came to Gail through a Doberman Pinscher rescue organization. From the start, Lacey Jane fell in love with her new owner. In her first obedience class, she refused treats, but she would do anything for Gail's praise. Shortly after graduating from the class, Gail received a call from a local hospital asking her to help set up a pet therapy program. (The training facility had recommended Gail and Lacey when the hospital had called them for help in finding volunteers.)

Gail and Lacey teamed up with a friend, Michelle, who had a yellow Labrador Retriever named Butter. The two dogs made the perfect pair—Butter entertained while Lacey consoled. The dogs started out in the Transitional Care Unit, then, once they proved their abilities, they were moved into the locked and unlocked psychiatric units. Lacey and Butter participated in the group therapy sessions, helping patients focus on grooming and training tasks. During each visit, Lacey worked the room until she found the neediest patient. Lacey consistently picked out the person who had had a particularly bad night or was especially depressed that day.

One day, Lacey watched a patient who refused to participate in the group session. Although Lacey had never left the meeting room before, when the patient walked out of the room, Lacey broke from the group and followed her. Gail let Lacey go and watched as she gingerly walked beside the patient, leaning gently against her until she stopped against the wall. Soon, the patient lowered her hand and began to stroke Lacey's head. After a moment, she slid down the wall and sat on the floor, then wrapped her arms around Lacey's neck. The two remained in that position for twenty minutes. Lacey never moved, standing still as a statue as she listened to the woman's whispered secrets. The next time Gail and Lacey arrived for group therapy, the patient was waiting expectantly at the elevators to groom Lacey and tell her more secrets. Staff members told Gail that since her initial "consult" with Lacey, the woman was participating with the group and had shown amazing progress.

On a visit to a different area of the hospital, Lacey and Gail met with a woman at the request of her son. Although the woman was in the final stage of her life and was not responsive, she had always loved animals, and the son felt she might be able to sense Lacey's presence on some level. Gail and the nurse lowered the metal bars and Lacey rested her muzzle on the bed. Gail picked up the woman's lifeless hand and made stroking motions on Lacey's soft head. When Gail let go, she was amazed to see the woman's hand continue to move. Suddenly the woman's eyes opened, and a frail voice asked, "What's her name?" Gail turned in time to see the head nurse leave the room, her eyes brimming with tears, to share this miracle with the other staff.

Gail says that while Lacey's compassion with patients is always awe-inspiring, she is truly mystified by another of the Doberman's abilities that she discovered one day while working in the transitional care unit. Lacey was uncharacteristically stubborn that day, and kept heading toward the lounge area. Gail tried to pull the Doberman into a patient's room, but Lacey refused to go. Gail finally gave up and let the leash go slack. Lacey entered the lounge and headed straight for a woman and her daughter, who were sitting at a table, crying. Gail apologized for interrupting and tried to pull Lacey back to the hallway. The woman stopped her and insisted Lacey stay, saying, "She knows we could use a pet now." As they hugged and patted Lacey's sleek body, a nurse walked in and told them she was sorry for their loss. Their mother/grandmother had died twenty minutes before Gail and Lacey had arrived.

"Somehow Lacey sensed this, and we were able to comfort the family," says Gail. "She has done this on three separate occasions, each time selecting an individual out of a crowd and refusing to go anywhere until she has done her job."

MEGAN

When Cheryl Weaver decided to pursue therapy work with her Rottweiler, she was determined to prove that the breed was not made up of vicious monsters, as is often portrayed by the media. Little did she realize the impact Megan would have on hundreds of lives during her decade of reaching out to others.

Cheryl remembers one day with special fondness. She and Megan were doing speech therapy with a woman who was recovering from a stroke and subsequent problems due to oxygen deprivation. When dinnertime arrived, the therapist mentioned how wonderful it would be if Megan could actually feed the patient. The woman was being fed through a tube, and the staff was trying to teach her how to eat again by feeding her applesauce.

Although Cheryl had taught Megan to hold almost anything in her mouth, she had never tried a spoon with food on it; Megan was known as a chowhound! But Cheryl went to the kitchen and found a spoon. She put some applesauce on the spoon and asked Megan to hold it in her mouth. Much to everyone's amazement, Megan obliged. Until then, the patient had been unable to move, but when Megan grabbed the spoon, the woman smiled. Cheryl saw the amusement in her eyes and knew if she could laugh, she would have.

As Megan gingerly stepped up onto the bench where the woman was sitting, the woman leaned forward slightly, opened her mouth, and then closed it on the spoon that was being held by the patient Rottweiler. Everyone in the room was stunned at the amazing progress Megan had prompted.

Later that evening, when asked if she had a good day, the woman sighed and very quietly uttered Megan's name; it was the first word she had spoken in more than three months.

Megan also had an amazing impact in the life of a little boy she visited weekly in a group home for mentally and sexually abused children. When he had his tonsils removed, the little boy asked for Megan instead of his mother. Upon returning to the home following surgery, the boy refused to take his medicine. The hospital instructed the therapists to bring him back to the hospital for IV fluid therapy, but the therapists decided to call Cheryl and Megan instead to see if they could help.

Megan seemed to understand what needed to be done. She crawled up on the couch with the child and laid her head on his chest. She swallowed so he could feel her throat on his chest, and then she swallowed again. "It was as if she knew what we wanted him to do and this was her way of showing him," says Cheryl.

The boy followed Megan's lead and swallowed. Soon he was sharing a Popsicle with the dog, and finally consented to take his medicine. Shortly afterward he fell asleep, with Megan by his side.

EXPO

Alice Linn of Birmingham, Alabama, tells how her Shetland Sheepdog, Expo, made a difference in the life of one young man.

It was Expo's very first therapy visit. Alice and Expo had already spent an hour visiting the occupational and physical therapy patients. They were getting ready to sign out when the therapists brought in a young man who was completely comatose, although not asleep. His eyes were dead looking, and he didn't respond to anything or anyone. The therapists asked if Alice would let him pet the dog. As several people held the young man in a sitting position, Alice placed Expo beside him. The therapists put the man's hand on Expo's back and just let it sit there. The man's hand remained still for several minutes as Alice and the therapists spoke to him. Suddenly, they saw the man's hand move, and he began to pet Expo. He ran his hand down Expo's leg and felt each toenail. Then he ran his hand up to Expo's head and felt his ears and his nose and then all over his body. Expo sat for forty-five minutes, never moving.

Alice says, "Although that was an exciting experience, what happened two weeks later sent chills up my spine. We were visiting again and saw the same young man. He was now sitting up with a sparkle in his eyes. He still couldn't communicate with anyone, but he could follow their directions and take an interest in things going on around him. He still had a long way to go, but the breakthrough came because of a little Sheltie who sat patiently by a broken man."

CHAPTER 3

CANINE HEROES

The dogs described in this chapter have taken their compassion to the next level, performing heroic feats that defy explanation. Time and again, dogs have risked their own lives to save their owners—or even strangers—who are in danger.

BOUDREAUX

Rescue workers are heroes to many dogs who are saved from the sad end that awaits them in animal shelters across the country. When a volunteer rescue worker from a Golden Retriever Rescue in Texas spotted what appeared to be a purebred black and mahogany Bloodhound at the Fort Worth Humane Society's shelter in 1996, she knew she was probably saving a dog's life. She never could have dreamed that this dog, in turn, would save many others.

The volunteer who originally rescued the eight-month-old Bloodhound was unable to keep him, and she passed him along to Sue Daniel, a fellow rescue worker. Because Sue and her husband, David, already owned eight dogs and were fostering two Goldens at the time, they had no intention of keeping the hound, so they actively searched for a suitable home. When Sue took one of the foster Goldens to the local police to receive training as a drug dog, she also took Boudreaux, thinking the police might be convinced to take the Bloodhound. Although the police told her they had no room in their K-9 program for Boudreaux at the time, they were impressed with his innate trailing ability.

Sue felt she was onto something and contacted several search and rescue organizations, but none showed an interest in adopting the hound. Finally, she called Walt Partin, who handled Bloodhound rescue for the south-central portion of the country. Walt politely suggested that perhaps Boudreaux already had the perfect home. This was all the excuse Sue needed, and Boudreaux officially became dog number nine in the Daniel pack.

Several months earlier, Sue read the book *So Others May Live* and became intrigued with the idea of search and rescue work. With Partin's prompting, she realized Boudreaux was presenting her with an opportunity to make this dream a reality. Sue and David embarked on a journey to turn Boudreaux into a full-fledged trailing dog.

Sue recalls the Bloodhound's occasional impatience with his novice owners' attempts at training. "Many times

David didn't think Boudreaux had taken the scent, and he would keep pulling Boudreaux closer to the scent article, telling him to check it. Boudreaux would bark as if to say, 'You idiot—I've got it!'"

David, Sue, and Boudreaux joined Search One Rescue Team of Dallas, Texas. This volunteer community search and rescue service organization assists government agencies in locating lost or missing persons. After months of intense training, Boudreaux finally became "mission ready" in April 1999. Boudreaux averages about two to three missions a month. His primary job is to locate the trail and establish the direction of travel to get the search team into the area of the missing person. Boudreaux has surpassed this role time after time, helping to rescue lost Alzheimer's patients, children, and people with mental disabilities throughout Texas and Oklahoma.

"He has a very strong natural desire to trail very successfully," David told a *Star-Telegram* newspaper reporter in September 2001. "Trailing dogs are not successful all the time, but his success rate is so high without making any mistakes that it's been phenomenal."

One example of Boudreaux's exceptional ability occurred in May 2001. An Alzheimer's patient had driven from Sherman, Texas, to Kemp, Oklahoma. His car was found stuck in the sand down a country road with a six-strand tight barbed wire fence on both sides of the road. Because the man was eighty-four years old, walked with a crutch, weighed 250 pounds, and had Alzheimer's, a heart condition, high blood pressure, and cancer, the sheriff believed the man never could have crossed the fence. The police thought the man must have gone one way or the other down the road. Boudreaux was cast around the abandoned car. After indicating three times to go through the fence, the bloodhound's handler decided to trust the dog's instincts, despite the police officers' skepticism.

They went through the fence and proceeded to work for more than an hour in a heavily wooded area. Boudreaux showed high interest in this area, and the handler suspected a strong scent pool. Boudreaux's handler stopped the Bloodhound for a rest and some water and requested that a team of searchers check out the area the dog had indicated. The Alzheimer's patient was found alive just 75 yards north of the scent pool area, after having been missing for three days. Without Boudreaux's expertise and persistence in following the track, the law enforcement officials most likely would have missed the man. Boudreaux's action gave rescuers the direction and area to search, which resulted in them finding the missing person and saving his life.

This is just one of the many amazing finds that earned Boudreaux the 2001 American Kennel Club Award for Canine Excellence (ACE) in the category of Search and Rescue Dog. A month later, the Bloodhound was honored again when he was inducted into the Texas Animal Hall of Fame. To receive an induction in the hero category, an animal must perform an incredible act of bravery or save a human life.

"Boudreaux changed our lives," says Sue. "He has given us challenges, rewards, laughter, and memories to last a lifetime. We feel fortunate to be the owners of the great 'hound from the pound.'"

BETH

Lynn Dumbrell of West Sussex, England, bought her Bearded Collie, Beth—otherwise known as Sunbree Such Delight—to work cattle on her farm. At the time, Lynn was relatively new to the world of dogs. Beth's breeder seemed to think Lynn was being overly optimistic in her plans for Beth, but Lynn had read that Bearded Collies were herding dogs, so she didn't think there would be any problem. Looking back, Lynn says she is amazed at her naïveté. That optimistic attitude, however, may have saved her life.

At the time, Lynn owned a rescued German Shepherd named Folly who, within a week of arriving at the farm, proved her ability to work cattle. Amazingly, Beth showed the same aptitude. She had a mind of her own and instinctively knew what to do and when to do it. Lynn said Beth made it clear she didn't need her owner butting in!

Beth's instincts were tested one day when a neighbor's herd of young Charollais cattle waded across the stream that divided the two properties.

"These Charollais—a very large European breed—were about twelve months old," says Lynn. "They had been single suckled and therefore were not used to being handled." Lynn found herself confronted with fifteen cattle, each weighing about a ton.

After thirty minutes of trying to convince the cattle to cross the stream back the way they had come, Lynn contemplated another approach. She and her neighbor decided to herd them down to the farm buildings. He would then get his truck and transport them home.

Beth drove the cattle according to plan, and eventually got them onto the track that led directly into the main cattle yard, where they would be secure. The track had four strands of barbed wire on either side that were overgrown with brambles, forming an impenetrable barrier. The men went ahead to open gates at the far end of the track, leaving Lynn and Beth at the back. Lynn marveled at how easily things were going when suddenly one of the metal gates crashed back against a wall. In one fluid movement, the entire herd turned and galloped straight back up the track toward Lynn and her dog. Lynn realized she had nowhere to go, and she couldn't outrun the frightened cattle.

As she braced herself to be trampled, a flash of fur shot out in front of her. Beth ran toward the cattle in short bursts, her legs stiffened and tail held high, barking with an urgent ferocity Lynn had never heard before. As the Charollais approached the dog, they started to slow. Beth pressed on. Lynn quickly sprang to action and began waving her arms and shouting as a backup to Beth's bark. The cattle finally halted about 10 yards from where Beth and Lynn stood. They turned around and, with Beth at their heels, walked back down the track and into the cattle yard.

Lynn's heart was racing, but Beth seemed nonplused by the danger she had just encountered. In fact she seemed quite proud, secure in the knowledge that she had proven herself a talented herding dog.

"I was quite shaken by the experience, but Beth had a good day," says Lynn. "I know that Beth saved my life.

"I lost Beth on July 1, 1999, and miss her dreadfully. She was a once-in-a-lifetime companion."

CHILLIE

When dogs perform acts of selflessness, they often receive a hero's reception. These uplifting stories are favorites for newspapers and as final pieces on the nightly news. Most of these courageous canines bask in the glory of the spotlight, then return home to the love of their families. Sadly, this was not the case for Chillie, a heroic Akita.

The morning of March 12, 1996, Miriam Rodriguez of New York City sent her two oldest children off to school. Her husband, Ignacio Vasquitelles, who is diabetic and had suffered a stroke, and their two younger children were still sleeping, so she decided to join them. She had just dozed off when she awoke to the sound of the family's eight-year-old Akita, Chillie, barking and scratching at the closed bedroom door. As she opened the door, she saw Chillie run to the children's room, pull the covers off their beds and nudge them insistently with her paw, trying to rouse them. Miriam saw flames racing through the kitchen. She awoke her husband, they grabbed the children, and they all fled out to the street with Chillie at their heels. Seconds later, an explosion caused by the electrical fire rocked their apartment, claiming the lives of the family's pet Chihuahua and cat.

The apartment was completely destroyed by the inferno. Miriam spent the next month in a hospital undergoing treatment for burns on her arms, back, and feet.

The family, who was now homeless, sought refuge at a rundown shelter in the Bronx.

Chillie was proclaimed a hero for saving her family's lives. Mayor Rudolph Giuliani awarded her a medallion and an official commendation for her actions. Pictures of the mayor standing with Chillie and the children she saved appeared in the local newspapers along with stories touting Chillie's courage.

Despite public acclaim for Chillie, however, officials at the homeless shelter ordered the family to get rid of the dog due to their strict "no dog" policy. The shelter filed a civil lawsuit to force the family to get rid of the Akita or face eviction.

The family's volunteer lawyer contended in court that because of his disability, Mr. Vasquitelles was entitled to keep Chillie in the family's shelter apartment under both the federal Fair Housing Act and the city's Civil Rights Act. The court ruled in the family's favor.

Finally the day came when the family was to leave the homeless shelter for more permanent housing. Sadly, they decided they could no longer afford to keep Chillie. The canine hero who had saved the family from certain death was turned in to an animal shelter with a notoriously high kill rate.

One of the workers recognized Chillie from the news stories. Eager to save the dog from being destroyed, she sent e-mails to every Akita rescue group and breeder that she could find, telling them of Chillie's plight.

One e-mail reached Akita Rescue of Western New York. As they read about the Akita's depressed demeanor as she waited on the shelter's death row, the rescue's director and vice president vowed to do something. Unfortunately, the rescue did not have any kennel space available, its volunteer foster homes were full, and the treasury was empty of funds. But the two women decided to use their own money to find Chillie a home. After numerous telephone calls and e-mails, Chillie was moved from the New York shelter to a temporary foster home in Pennsylvania. They publicized Chillie's plight in the hopes of finding a permanent home for the Akita, but privately they worried about her future. It would be difficult to find someone willing to take on an 8-year-old dog.

Meanwhile, across the country, Hogan Sung of San Francisco was surfing the Internet as he built a memorial Web page for his deceased Bulldog, who coincidentally also was named Chillie. After typing the name "Chillie" into a search engine, he found the rescue organization's Web page on Chillie the Akita. He was touched by the dog's story and decided immediately that she should be part of his family. He flew 3,000 miles to meet her and bring her back home to California.

This seems like a happy ending to a fairy-tale story, but Chillie once again found herself facing a life-threatening situation. Shortly after Hogan adopted Chillie, she developed bloat, a potentially fatal condition in which a dog's stomach suddenly fills with gas. Hogan believes the bloat was caused by Chillie's stress at losing the only family she had ever known. Determined not to lose his newfound companion, Hogan drained his savings to pay for her surgery. Although age was against her, Chillie recovered fully. Today, she lives happily with Hogan, another Akita rescue dog, and a rescued Bulldog.

Hogan says, "There were many great people involved with saving this angel Akita. I thank all involved and thank God every day for allowing me to be Chillie's guardian."

In 2001, Chillie received the American Kennel Club's Award for Canine Excellence (ACE) in the category of Exemplary Companion Dog. No one who has ever met this amazing dog would dispute that title.

TESSA

While we often hear stories of dogs saving their families, occasionally a dog comes to the rescue of someone it barely knows. Such is the case of Tessa, a German Shepherd–Collie mix who saved the life of her neighbor in November 2001.

One day, Mary Ann Michels, who is a hypnotherapist, came home to her one-room cabin in Auburn, California, determined to meditate. She put a pot of brown rice on the stove to simmer for fifty minutes, then turned off both phones and her answering machine. She sat down on a pile of pillows on the floor and soon was in a state of deep meditation.

After some time, she became aware of a dog barking somewhere outside. She tried to ignore it, but the dog kept barking. At first she was annoyed at this intrusion on her silence. "Then I thought, 'This is one of God's creatures,'" says Mary Ann. "I decided to use the dog's bark to help me reach a deeper state of meditation."

With each subsequent bark, Mary Ann went deeper into her subconscious. Then suddenly, she became aware of the dog's presence close by. It sounded as if the dog was on the steps right outside her window.

"By now the dog's bark was frantic, and I thought something must be wrong," says Mary Ann. Mary Ann began bringing herself back to full consciousness and glanced at the clock. Forty minutes had passed. She figured the rice was almost done. As she took a deep breath, she was struck by a pungent odor. She quickly realized that the flame on the stove had gone out, and her cabin was filled with gas.

Mary Ann rushed to the door and flung it open, breathing in the fresh air. As she appeared in the doorway, the dog, whom she recognized as belonging to a neighbor, abruptly stopped its frenzied barking and walked away.

"The dog saved my life," says Mary Ann. "Not only could I have passed out from the gas, but if the furnace had gone on, my cabin would have blown up with me inside."

Mary Ann was so shaken by the experience that she couldn't talk about it at first. She often thought about the dog that had saved her, but she was too awestruck about the experience to approach the dog's owners. She also was due to leave on a trip that she had been extremely nervous about. Mary Ann says the dog's actions that day actually helped ease her mind about her travels.

"This trip required me to take eight different planes. Because of September 11, I was pretty nervous, but after this dog saved me, I wasn't nervous anymore. I decided this was God's way of saying it wasn't my time yet. It didn't matter how many planes I was on; I knew I would be safe."

After returning home, Mary Ann decided it was time to properly thank the dog who had saved her life. Right before Christmas, Mary Ann showed up on her neighbor's doorstep with a basket of dog food and gourmet dog biscuits. Mary Ann explained to the puzzled owner what had happened.

"The owner told me the dog, named Tessa, wasn't a barker, but that she had barked the same way one time when the flame on their stove had gone out and she had smelled gas," says Mary Ann. "I am so in awe that Tessa was there for me when I needed her. She's my guardian angel."

CHANCE

Chance, a Rottweiler mix, is Paula Shepard's service dog. While most people have heard of dogs that assist people who are blind, deaf, or have a physical disability, Chance is somewhat unique in that he assists Paula with a hidden disorder.

Paula suffers from bipolar I disorder with affective features. She experiences mood swings and trouble with concise linear thinking. At times, her brain "shorts out," and she can't remember her own name. She occasionally hallucinates and experiences panic attacks. Paula's condition is resistant to medication, making treatment more difficult. Because of her condition, Paula rarely left the house except for necessary errands. She had no friends and no outside interests or hobbies. Her fear kept her from taking even short trips in the car by herself.

Chance was born in Paula's apartment after Paula saved his mother from an abusive home. Paula began training Chance from puppyhood to help her deal with her disorder, although at the time she didn't realize she was training him to be a service dog. Chance performs numerous duties to give Paula the emotional and physical assistance to pursue a normal life. Some of his duties include bracing Paula if she becomes disoriented, weak, or loses balance; nudging or patting Paula to rouse her when she disassociates or withdraws from reality; carrying medical supplies, a cell phone, and emergency information in a backpack; helping Paula distinguish a hallucination from reality by scanning the environment for anything out of the ordinary; keeping Paula's children grouped together, especially if Paula is having a bad spell and hasn't noticed that a child has wandered off; and keeping Paula calm when she becomes emotionally overwhelmed by laying his head in her lap or leaning close.

"All the things he does have the overall effect of grounding me and making me feel calm and safe so that I can function better," says Paula. "My brain is not reliable and gives me faulty information, so I look to him for confirmation of what my brain is telling me and assistance controlling the anxiety and extreme emotions that affect my everyday functioning."

One night, Chance rose above his usual duties to save the life he so willingly serves. Paula was temporarily staying in a motel in a bad part of town. She put her three children to bed, and after watching a bit of television, she drifted off to sleep. Sometime later, she groggily awoke to the enraged snarls of Chance and her two other dogs, a pit bull mix and a Bullmastiff. Only half-awake, Paula sternly told the dogs to be quiet. They settled down, and Paula drifted back to sleep, only to be awakened again moments later by furious barking followed by a brief silence. Slowly, Paula became aware of her surroundings and noticed a crack of light from her partially opened hotel room door. The dogs again barked frantically, and the door closed quickly as the dogs hit it, scratching and clawing at an unseen intruder. The dogs went silent, and the door creaked open again.

Paula gripped the blankets around her as she tried to understand what was happening. As the door opened, the dogs again hit it with all their strength. Paula cried out, "Dogs, who is that? Watch 'em!" The children across the room stirred, but did not awaken. At Paula's command, the dogs burst into a continuous frenzy at the door. Paula stumbled around the room, searching for her clothes, then quickly slipped them on.

As she cautiously approached the door, she noticed an electrical cord had slipped under the door and prevented it from closing all the way. At that moment, the door was opening again. Paula gained courage from the dogs' obvious intent to protect their family. She ordered the dogs to be quiet and get behind her. She opened the door to find a large man pulling his hand back from the doorknob. He stood there rather unsteadily, looking at her with glazed eyes. Paula trembled as she felt a lump rise in her throat. The Bullmastiff pressed against the back of her right leg, Chance pressed against the back of her left ankle, and the pit bull was behind her. They were silent, tensed, and ready for the next command.

"What do you think you are doing?" Paula asked loudly.

"I live here," the man mumbled.

"I don't think so," Paula countered, now annoyed as well as afraid. "This is my room, and I think I know who lives here."

The man shuffled his feet for a moment, and then said, "I'm the manager, and I need to come in and look at your bathroom."

"I don't think so," Paula stated. "I know the manager, and you're not him. You need to leave!"

"Okay," he mumbled, but he just stood there for several moments.

"Maybe you didn't understand me. I said, you need to leave, now!"

Paula pressed her leg into Chance and put her hand out behind her to signal that she needed his reassurance and comfort. She felt his wet nose, then his face under her trembling hand. She stroked him, gaining courage as she waited for the man to leave. She glanced at the children, who were now partially awake rubbing their eyes and trying to make sense of the scene before them. Paula nudged the pit bull with her foot and pointed behind her to the children as she kept her eyes on the man. Paula heard the dog jumping up on the children's bed. She gave a hand signal to the other dogs to stay behind her. If the man got past her and the two dogs, at least the pit bull would protect the children.

The man leaned against the walkway railing, making no move to leave. Then he said, "So, what are you doing? You're sure looking good tonight. Why don't I come in?"

He again stepped toward Paula. Another shock of terror raced through her as her hand moved from Chance's head down his neck to grasp his collar. She felt him tense further as he began to rumble under his breath.

"Apparently you didn't hear me. I said 'leave now!'"

The man shuffled another half step toward Paula.

"Let me introduce you to my dog!" Paula yelled, as she moved to the side, clearing the way for Chance, who squeezed past her with a menacing snarl. Paula straddled the dog, holding his collar as he lunged toward the man. The intruder recoiled against the railing, "Okay, okay. I'm leaving." He moved to the stairs leading down to the parking lot.

Paula shut and locked the door, then dropped to the floor. She grabbed Chance and held onto him fiercely as she felt the room swirl around her and reality fading in and out. Chance stayed by her side, licking her face and nudging her with his nose until the panic attack subsided and Paula could think clearly enough to call the police. When the officers arrived, the man was staggering around the parking lot, trying to break into cars.

If not for the brave actions of Chance and his canine "brothers," it is doubtful that Paula would have been able to defend herself and her children. It is very likely that Chance saved their lives that night, adding heroism to the list of amazing tasks he performs for those he loves.

AUSTIN

In her capacity as development director for Texas Hearing and Service Dogs (THSD), Cathie Newitt has met many extraordinary dogs. One in particular, however, stands out for his incredible ability to overcome abandonment and live the rest of his life serving people who need him.

A group of hunters discovered the Golden Retriever in the woods. The dog was dirty and starving, so they turned him in to Houston Golden Retriever Rescue. The rescue group contacted THSD's training director, who glimpsed real potential in the skinny dog with soft almost human brown eyes. Cathie brought the dog, now called Cash, home, gave him a bath and a good meal, then set about turning him into a service dog.

Cash had completed his training and was about to be paired with a disabled client when THSD received a call from the Austin Police Department. They were looking for a gentle search and rescue dog and were hoping the organization could help. As much as they hated to give up Cash, THSD felt he would be ideal for the job. Not only was he a quick learner, but he also loved to find anything that was lost, and he was comfortable crawling on his belly over any type of surface. THSD told the police department they could take Cash, on the condition that they could supervise the training and ensure that only positive conditioning methods were used.

Cash was renamed Austin to honor his new hometown, and he was paired with Officer Jim Minton, a rookie in the police canine division. Officer Minton and Austin were first called into service when a child disappeared from a restaurant parking lot. Austin arrived on the scene and immediately tracked the child through the parking lot and over to a nearby auto showroom, where the girl was found safe. She told Officer Minton she was looking for friends and had become thirsty. The policeman was overcome with pride as he realized that he and his dog had accomplished their goal as a team.

Once certified, Austin worked steadily with Officer Minton, answering ten to fifteen calls a month. On November 18, 1999, Austin received his most important assignment to date. Every year, students at nearby Texas A & M spend weeks constructing an enormous wood pile, then set fire to the Texas Aggie Bonfire before the annual football game against the University of Texas. This year's pile—which was 59 feet high and was engineered from approximately 5,000 logs, some weighing as much as 1,600 pounds—had collapsed, trapping people inside. Austin and Officer Minton, as the only canine tracking team brought in for the recovery effort, rushed to the scene.

Once they arrived, the team waited for engineers to determine if the log pile was stable enough to permit Austin to begin his search. At 5:30 P.M., three hours after the collapse, the equipment was silenced. Austin was lowered by hoist into a cavelike opening in the collapsed pile and was set down approximately 25 feet below the top of the pile into a ground-level void that the rescuers termed "the vault." Officer Minton was worried as he watched his best friend and partner disappear into the rubble, knowing the dog could be crushed if the pile were to give way. For several long minutes, Officer Minton watched for Austin to reappear at the top of the pile. Finally, he saw his soot-covered partner reemerge, a white baseball cap held firmly in his jaws. Officer Minton showered Austin with praise, then, with more than a little trepidation, gave Austin a second command to search. Several more minutes passed before Austin returned again, this time with a bloody helmet. Having determined the pile was stabilized, Officer Minton joined his canine partner, and the two entered the black void together, where he quickly spotted two deceased victims.

For the next two hours, crews removed 10-foot deep sections of logs to reduce and expose the pile. Afterward, Austin and his handler conducted a fresh perimeter search. Officer Minton reported to the rescue crews that he was certain no live victims remained, and the disaster site should be converted from a "search and rescue" to a "search and recovery" mission.

Austin conducted a total of four successful search missions that day. His work enabled rescue crews to determine how many victims were trapped, where they were located, and whether they were alive or dead. Twelve people were killed and twenty-seven were injured in the collapsed bonfire.

Cathie is still amazed that a dog that had been abandoned would be willing to place himself in such danger to help strangers in need. She points out that he not only was rehabilitated and retrained once, but twice, each time throwing himself with gusto into his appointed tasks.

But Austin's resume doesn't end there. In addition to being a high-achieving member of the Austin Police Department, Austin is also a "spokesdog" for the agency. When he's not out finding lost children and Alzheimer's patients who have wandered off, he and his partner do demonstrations at elementary schools and for service groups. Austin even helped raise much of the funding to equip his canine coworkers with bulletproof vests.

Austin's most recent achievement was receiving the American Kennel Club's Award of Canine Excellence (ACE) in its inaugural year, 2000. A nationwide search was conducted, with only four winners chosen. The mayor of Austin recognized this amazing dog by proclaiming October 26, 2000, as "Austin the Dog Day." In addition, the Texas Veterinary Medical Association inducted Austin into its Animal Hall of Fame on November 14, 2000.

Cathie says, "Those of us who know and love Austin were not at all surprised by his successes. We're all convinced there's probably nothing this dog can't do."

BEN

Most service dogs are raised from puppyhood with their future vocation in mind. They are placed with people who acquaint them with all types of situations and distractions they will encounter on the job, such as busy city streets, elevators, and wheelchairs. As they approach adulthood, they are trained for specific jobs, such as retrieving household items and opening doors for the handicapped. It is rare for a dog who has not received this specialized training to learn "on the job" how to handle the challenges of being a service dog. Ben is one of these rare exceptions, which makes his story even more remarkable.

When she was twenty-five, Karen Shirk of Batavia, Ohio, was diagnosed with Myasthenia Gravis, a neuromuscular disease. At the time, she was a graduate student in social work who at first blamed her fatigue on the demands of juggling college and a job. Soon, however, she began to stumble, then experienced difficulty breathing. When she finally sought medical help, the diagnosis was devastating. Within six months, she couldn't breath without the help of a ventilator. Over the next six years, as treatment after treatment failed, Karen gave up on life and hoped each day would be her last. If only she could find some glimmer of hope, she thought, maybe she could find a way to go on. The hope she was searching for was a medical cure. Instead, the hope she found was in the form of a 30-pound bundle of black fur.

In 1992, a friend suggested that perhaps a service dog would decrease Karen's dependence on home care and allow her some privacy. Karen applied for a service dog and began the long wait. After a year, she received a call telling her the agency had a possible match and that a staff member would visit her for a final interview. Several weeks later, Karen was devastated to learn that the agency wouldn't place a dog with a person who used a ventilator.

"That day, I began to plan for my death," says Karen. "I would not sit and wait for death to come, I would go to it willingly."

Her friend suggested that Karen look at puppies. Karen humored her by visiting several litters, but each time she voiced her fears that if she couldn't care for herself, how could she care for a puppy? One day, Karen's friend called in response to a newspaper ad advertising German Shepherd puppies for sale. The puppies' parents weren't show dogs; instead, they had dedicated their lives to a man with Crohn's disease. When Karen's friend asked if the puppies would grow big enough and strong enough to assist a woman who used a wheelchair, the man responded, "These dogs could pull a wheelchair across the United States when they grow up." He offered to sell Karen a puppy for half price if she were interested. Karen agreed to see the puppies, although she was skeptical.

"I watched the dogs play, but I was set in my resolve to die," she says. "Then, there he was; this giant black ball of fur, all feet and ears, sitting and watching me. I'm not sure what happened that day, but our eyes met, and he went home with me."

Immediately, Ben showed an amazing aptitude to learn the tasks Karen asked of him. As Ben assisted in her day-to-day life, Karen's spirits lifted. As she allowed herself to feel happiness, her body reacted. She began to respond to a new treatment and started on the slow path back to an active life.

Two years after acquiring Ben, Karen took her companion to National K-9 in Columbus, where he learned to perform specialized tasks that he hadn't been able to figure out on his own. He already was able to help Karen undress, retrieve items she dropped, and block an elevator door so it wouldn't close on his owner. At National K-9, Ben learned to retrieve consistently, to answer the phone, to pull a wheelchair, to pull Karen out of a chair, and to retrieve Karen's special bag that contains lifesaving medication. After four months of training, Ben graduated and earned his Ohio assistance dog license.

In 1996, with Ben at her side, Karen got a job at an agency serving disabled children and mentally challenged adults. She worked at Stepping Stones as a program manager in the Adult Day Habilitation Program. Ben often helped with physical therapy, standing just far enough away from a patient so that he or she was forced to stretch muscles to reach out and pet him. In 1998, Karen founded 4 Paws for Ability, Inc., which places assistance dogs with the disabled. She now uses her neuromuscular disease and her struggles to share with others all that Ben has brought to her life. In January 2001, Ben and Karen returned to college, where Karen is working to complete her Master's degree in Social Work.

Despite the training Ben received at National K-9, his instincts often take over when needed the most. One day, Karen experienced a medical emergency and needed to get her medication into her bloodstream immediately. It had never occurred to her, however, that if she weren't able to breathe, she also wouldn't be able to speak. Since she is careful to never be far from her special medical bag, she turned in her chair to see where it was, then gave Ben a hand signal to retrieve it.

"What a surprise to see it right in front of me hanging from Ben's mouth before I even had a chance to ask for it," says Karen. "He knew me so well that my needs were his needs. I would never be afraid of living with this disease again."

This wasn't the only time Ben saved Karen's life. In 2000, Karen underwent open-heart surgery twice in seventy-two hours. Soon after returning home from the hospital, Karen experienced a reaction to a medication combination that left her unconscious and in serious condition. Ben stayed by her side, keeping a constant vigil. When Karen's father called to check on her, Ben picked up the phone and brought it to his owner, but Karen was unable to take it. Knowing something was wrong, Ben dropped the phone on the chair and started barking into it. Karen's father, who lives more than an hour away, immediately called the police and reported that it sounded as if the dog had picked up the phone, then laid it close enough to Karen's face to let him hear his daughter's irregular breathing. He told the police that the German Shepherd hesitated before he began barking, as if he wanted to make sure Karen's breathing was audible. Ben was still barking ten minutes later when the first police officer arrived.

"Some service dogs are trained to hit 911 buttons and/or lifelines," Karen says. "Ben was not. Although he has always retrieved the phone when asked to do so, he was not trained to do it automatically."

Ben has received many awards for his amazing work. He won the Purina Mills "Why I Love My Pet" contest in 1996 and the Miejer Star Search contest in 1997. In 1998, he was one of the Delta Society's Beyond Limits National Service Dog Award winners, and in 2001 he received a Special Services Award from the organization for saving Karen's life. Ben also competes in obedience trials and has completed two of the three legs necessary to earn a Companion Dog title from the American Kennel Club.

Although Karen will never be completely free from this devastating disease, she has made incredible progress in regaining her independence. Today, Karen only uses a ventilator at night and has home care services for just a few hours a day.

"With Ben at my side, a power wheelchair, and a modified van, I am living every day just the way I want to, and I wouldn't change a thing," says Karen. "Time and time again Ben is the driving force in my life. When I fall into self-pity over the difficulties in life or over an ability that the disease has robbed me of, Ben refuses to allow me to wallow in it. He gets into my bag and brings me the van keys as if he were saying, 'Okay, that's enough. Let's get on with life!' There is nothing this disease can throw at me that Ben and I will not find a way to overcome."

BO

Bo, an Australian Cattledog mix, has been Mary Rook's service/guide dog for three years. On July 19, 2001, he proved that when confronted by danger, he would willingly serve as her protector as well.

That morning, Bo and Mary were out for their morning stroll in Seattle, Washington. Mary is physically and visually impaired. Bo serves as Mary's "eyes" and allows her to move about independently, although she is confined to a wheelchair. Mary remembers relaxing in her wheelchair with her hand resting on Bo's harness. As the two traveled down the street, Mary breathed in the scent of blooming flowers and enjoyed the splashes of color.

Suddenly, she detected unusual movement through the harness. Bo seemed to be looking back over his shoulder at something. Thinking it was an oncoming car, Mary signaled Bo to help her move over to the side of the road so the car could drive by. They moved over, but Mary quickly noticed there was no sound of a motor from a car, and no accompanying breeze from a car passing by. Bo continued to look over his shoulder.

Mary felt a shiver of fear run through her as she realized what might have put Bo on alert—a stray dog, perhaps intent on picking a fight. A moment after she had the thought, a dog suddenly appeared at her right side. Mary quickly turned her power wheelchair to the left in an attempt to keep the dog from reaching Bo.

Then the attack began. Mary realized she had underestimated the danger. They were being attacked by not one, but two dogs—dogs that she would later find out were pit bulls.

The dogs each grabbed one end of Bo in their jaws and picked him up in the air, then savagely tugged him back and forth between them as if he were a stuffed toy. Mary knew her precious Bo was no match for the wild dogs.

Since Mary doesn't have much feeling in her hands, Bo is actually harnessed to her body so she can feel his movements more easily. As the attack progressed, she felt herself being shaken violently. If she hadn't been wearing a seatbelt, she would have been dragged to the ground and probably mauled as well.

After several more minutes, the pit bulls dropped Bo and one began to viciously bite the wheelchair. Mary was desperate; since she was being attacked from both sides, she couldn't turn away, and she knew she couldn't outrun the dogs.

Sensing his owner's danger, Bo staggered to his feet and threw himself between Mary and the dogs. Time and again he pushed himself between his owner and whichever dog was closest, doing his best to fend off their attack. The dogs' attention once again returned to Bo, and they continued their relentless assault, even jumping onto Mary's chair to come at Bo from another angle with their teeth. Mary sat helplessly in her wheelchair and screamed for help.

After what seemed like hours, but was later determined to be about fifteen minutes, a young man rushed over and got between the dogs and Mary and Bo. He managed to keep them at bay until their owner arrived and got them under control.

Deep bite marks on Bo, his harness, and the wheelchair itself were testament to the brutal attack. Although he required surgery and several weeks to recover, Bo soon was back on duty.

"In true Cattledog style, Bo has returned to his job as my service/guide dog, and we are again able to conduct seminars for the Northwest Aide Dog Foundation at schools and libraries, educating students about the importance of aide dogs working with people with disabilities," says Mary. "Bo is definitely my furry hero!"

GINGER

Ginger's heroic story was first reported in Dogs For Dignity, the official newsletter of Paws With a Cause (PAWS), an organization that trains and places service dogs.

Ginger, a black Labrador Retriever, was donated to PAWS by Richard Oetting of Grand Rapids, Michigan. Ginger had already begun her training to be a hearing/service dog when Rosemary Douglas submitted an application for a canine companion. Rosemary specifically asked for a dog that was trained to alert her to a smoke alarm and an intruder. She was especially afraid of her inability to hear these sounds since her husband often worked nights and they lived in a dangerous area. Rosemary's disability prevented her from moving quickly to get to safety. Rosemary and Ginger were paired together in 1990 and were certified as a team by the end of that year.

Ginger soon proved not only a capable assistant, but a heroic protector as well. During one week in 1991, Ginger alerted Rosemary and her husband twice to an intruder at their home. Not long after, she also saved Rosemary from two young muggers.

"I took Ginger to the mall on a Sunday afternoon to practice holding the doors open for me," says Rosemary. "When we got to the parking lot after walking around the mall for a while, Ginger started to growl and would not walk any closer to our car. I looked around to see what she was growling about when two teenaged boys jumped out from between two cars. One grabbed my purse and the other was going to hit me with a stick. Ginger jumped up and grabbed the boy's wrist and he dropped my purse. The stick that was meant for my head landed on Ginger's back. She went down for a minute, but seemed okay because she had her backpack on. The boys took off, and I checked Ginger to see if she was all right. Then she got my purse and all the small things that fell out of it and gave them to me without me even asking!"

While PAWS does not train assistance dogs to provide protection, Ginger's reaction to the muggers was proof of her bond with Rosemary and her commitment to serving her partner.

For the next nine years, Ginger proved herself a hero to Rosemary in smaller, yet significant ways by helping Rosemary maintain her independence and peace of mind on a daily basis. Then, on the evening of September 19, 2000, Ginger again placed herself in danger to protect Rosemary and her husband. This time, however, she made the ultimate sacrifice for her beloved owners.

Rosemary was working in her sewing room when Ginger tried to get her attention. When Rosemary didn't understand what Ginger was trying to tell her and didn't respond the way Ginger wanted, the Lab became extremely agitated and ran around Rosemary's wheelchair, then tugged at her pants. Finally Rosemary realized something was wrong. She followed Ginger to the kitchen, where a fire had broken out. As she opened the door to escape outside, an influx of air caused an explosion that propelled Rosemary and Ginger out of the house. Ginger staggered to her feet and rushed to check on Rosemary, who had been thrown from her wheelchair. Once she saw that her owner was okay, she rushed back into the house to look for Rosemary's husband, who was normally home from work by that time, but was running late that day.

When firefighters arrived and entered the house, they found Ginger collapsed on the floor next to Rosemary's husband's bed. Despite their efforts, they were unable to resuscitate Ginger.

"Obviously, devastating sorrow was first felt by the staff of PAWS, as it is a tragedy for any animal to die in such a way," stated the newsletter. "The sadness was eased a bit, however, as our pride and respect grew for this wonderful dog. PAWS may have trained her, but it was her partnership with and devotion to Rosemary that made her a hero."

VALENTINE

June Beech's hearing dog, Valentine, makes an impact on June's life every day by alerting her to sounds she otherwise would not be able to hear. June received the mixed breed through Hearing Dogs for Deaf People, a charitable organization based in the United Kingdom. Although Valentine has only lived with June at her home in England for a year, she has already proven herself indispensable.

Valentine helps June on a daily basis by alerting her to jangling telephones, whistling teakettles, ringing doorbells, and other sounds. She is trained to react to noises by finding June, sitting in front of her, and touching her on the leg with a paw. When June opens her hands and asks, "What is it?" Valentine leads her to the source of the sound. If the sound is a fire or smoke alarm, Valentine is trained to tap June with her paw, but when June asks about the sound, Valentine then lies down to indicate danger. Although Valentine has been trained to perform these tasks, the dog has reacted beyond her everyday duties, proving that her actions are not just trained responses, but genuine compassion for her owner and family.

On the first occasion, June was out in the garden and Valentine was lying nearby. Suddenly, Valentine disappeared. When the dog returned, she touched June with her paw as a signal and tried to lead her owner back into the house. At first June didn't react. Valentine kept pestering June and became increasingly frantic. Finally, June realized the dog was trying to tell her something important. When June followed Valentine into the house, she found her father-in-law lying on the floor, the victim of a stroke. June quickly called for an ambulance.

Valentine had heard the man collapse and had come in to investigate. Acting on her own initiative, she alerted June, knowing her owner would be able to help. If it weren't for Valentine, precious time may have elapsed before June discovered her fallen father-in-law. Valentine's quick reaction possibly saved his life.

Several months later, Valentine once again proved her love and concern for her newly adopted family. "Valentine had just come home after a three-day stay at the vet's due to a viral form of gastroenteritis, and she was doing quite poorly," says June. "The vet told me not to work her for three to four days so she could get her strength back. The day after Valentine came home, she came up to me and touched me with her paw. I thought she was looking for attention, not alerting me. But she persisted as if to say, 'Come on—you're needed!'"

June followed Valentine and found her husband, Stephen, lying on the patio outside, where he had collapsed from a suspected brain hemorrhage.

"I couldn't believe that she had done it again," says June. "If it weren't for Valentine, who knows how long Stephen could have been lying there. She is my champion wonder dog."

But that wasn't the last of Valentine's heroic actions. She also saved June from a potentially deadly accident.

"I was crossing the road between two lorries (trucks)," says June. "I shouldn't have crossed there, but I wasn't thinking. I said to Valentine, 'Come on, heel,' then tried to cross, but she wouldn't move. She just kept backing toward the pavement. I tried a couple of times, but she still refused to budge, and then another lorry came whizzing past. I just couldn't believe my eyes. I wouldn't have heard it! I stepped back onto the pavement and gave her a huge hug, with tears rolling down my cheeks. Valentine had done it again."

Newspapers and the Internet are filled with stories of even more dogs who have risked their lives to save others.

- Sophie, a deaf Dalmatian, saved five-year-old Georgia from drowning when the girl fell into a fast-flowing swollen river. Although Sophie couldn't hear Georgia's screams, when she saw the girl struggling, the dog plunged into the water and swam to the girl. Georgia hung on to Sophie as the dog paddled back to the river's edge. Georgia's mother rushed to the bank and helped the girl and the dog out of the water.

- A stray dog saved an abandoned baby from certain death during a freezing winter day in Romania. The dog stood guard over the child, who had been left in a public park, and barked and howled until people stopped to investigate. They found the baby girl hidden in a plastic bag under a picnic table. The baby, whose umbilical cord was still attached, was sent to the hospital to recover, and the maternity unit adopted the dog.

- Biyou, a three-year-old Australian Shepherd mix, saved her owner from drowning in an icy creek and freezing from exposure. Lisa Parker of Richmond Dale, Ohio, was attempting to free her horse, who had slipped down a steep bank and broken through the ice, when she also fell into the freezing water. Biyou rushed to her owner and pulled Lisa through the icy water until she was able to roll herself onto the ice shelf. Biyou prodded and pawed at Lisa to keep her moving as she climbed the near vertical embankment. When Lisa reached the top, she collapsed from exhaustion and the weight of her layers of wet, frozen clothing. Biyou licked her face until she gathered the strength to stagger the 200 yards to her house. Biyou was awarded the Skippy Dog Hero of the Year Award in 2001, offered by Heinz Pet Products, for saving Lisa's life.

- Ursula Strider, of Waynesboro, Virginia, adopted Dover from an English Setter rescue group, which took in the dog after he suffered head injuries from being hit by a truck. In return, Dover prevented Ursula's two-year-old daughter from being bitten by a snake. Dover suffered severe bites to his face when he positioned himself between the snake and the toddler, but he made a full recovery. Dover was named a 2001 runner up in the Skippy Dog Hero of the Year Awards for his heroism.

- Mixed-breeds Stella and Mo were hiking with their owner, Kellee, in a park when six pit bulls approached them and began attacking the dogs. When Kellee tried to save her pets, the pit bulls turned on her. Stella fought the dogs, giving Kellee and Mo a chance to escape. When Stella tried to follow them, the pit bulls again tried to attack Kellee. Stella got between Kellee and the marauding dogs and refused Kellee's command to come. Stella continued to fight the pack of dogs while Kellee and Mo ran to get help. Sadly, Stella died from her injuries. She is the first dog to be recognized posthumously by the Skippy Dog Hero of the Year Awards, which named her a runner up in 2001.

CHAPTER 4

DOGS OF SEPTEMBER 11

When the World Trade Center and Pentagon were hit by terrorist attacks on September 11, 2001, hundreds of dogs from across the country heeded the call to action. Police K-9s, volunteer search and rescue dogs, and trained therapy dogs arrived from near and far to help with the rescue efforts.

Although some may argue that these dogs were simply doing what they are trained to do, those at the scene know that the dogs were doing much more than that. Even though they were confronted with an unstable environment of shifting, smoldering rubble, the dogs approached their task with unwavering determination. Every dog who worked the first few days at Ground Zero faced choking smoke and ash and intense heat. Despite these hardships, they just kept working. Often, the dogs lost their footing on twisted metal and concrete, and several were hurt by falls. Still, they shook themselves off and jumped back into the fray, working until they were ready to drop from exhaustion and their handlers had to pull them off the job for their own safety.

As the work went on and no survivors were found, the experience took a toll on the dogs. Many became visibly depressed and found comfort only in their ability to comfort others. Although we can teach a dog the basics of searching for a human being, we cannot teach this overwhelming compassion—it comes from the heart.

CHARLIE

When Suzanne McCrosson first got word of the World Trade Center attack, she knew exactly what she needed to do. Suzanne, who is one of only five female police officers in the New York City Police Department's thirty-four-member emergency services canine unit, grabbed her canine partner, Charlie, and headed to Ground Zero.

Although Charlie and Suzanne had been working partners for three years before September 11, neither the black German Shepherd nor the seasoned officer had ever encountered such a monumental task.

Charlie is extremely versatile. In his capacity as a patrol dog, he uses scent to find lost children or criminals hiding in buildings. But like many of the police dogs at the scene, the smoldering, shifting rubble at the World Trade Center presented challenges he had never encountered. Many times, Charlie, who was used to working on the level streets of New York City, effortlessly walked across beams with 20-foot drops on either side. Despite his lack of training for such a situation, Charlie approached the job with eager determination.

"He used the same skills he already has to track down a bad guy, but without the aggression," says Suzanne. "That's where our teamwork really came into play. I could tell from his body language and his bark if he had found something."

When he located a scent, the 95-pound Shepherd let out a booming bark and began to dig frantically. At Charlie's signal, Suzanne pulled him off the rubble and human recovery personnel moved in to continue the search. In his time at Ground Zero, Charlie located two victims, but sadly he was unable to find anyone alive.

Although many search and rescue dogs at the scene showed signs of depression at the lack of live finds, Charlie never lost his eagerness for the search. "We have a saying in the department that emotions travel down lead," says Suzanne. "Whatever the handler is feeling usually translates down the leash to the dog. Although we were horrified by what we were witnessing, as police officers, we are trained to hold our emotions in check. But most of the search and rescue teams from around the country that joined the effort are just regular people who do this because of their love for their dogs and their desire to help. They are teachers or grocery store workers who use their own money to travel across the country to train and lend a hand in a catastrophe. They are well trained for search and rescue, but as civilians, they aren't prepared for the emotional shock they may experience and the gruesome sights they may see. Understandably, they get very upset, and this is communicated down to their dogs."

Suzanne admits, however, that despite their training, even the most hardened police officers and firefighters found it difficult to remain emotionless in the face of such devastation. "Even handlers who had taken their dogs to Oklahoma City or to different disaster sites around the world just shook their heads when they saw Ground Zero." Suzanne adds, "The sheer devastation was incomprehensible."

Suzanne says the area had an unreal quality to it, as if it were a movie set. While uptown Manhattan remained untouched and looked as it did on any other day, lower Manhattan was a war zone. No one knew quite how to deal with such a disastrous attack. Each day, as Suzanne and Charlie arrived on the scene to work, they met countless people walking around dazed.

Often they would have to wait until a certain area was stabilized before it was safe for them to begin their search. That was when Suzanne witnessed the phenomenal effect that Charlie and the other dogs had on the seasoned workers who were trying so hard to be strong.

"Many of the rescue workers were walking around like zombies," Suzanne says. "They were trying to be calm and just go about their jobs, when inside they were dealing with all these horrible emotions. When they saw the dogs, their whole demeanor changed. All they wanted to do was pet the dogs. It was therapy for them to get something as simple as a paw shake or kiss from one of these dogs."

Suzanne notes that usually people don't want to come near a police dog, especially Charlie who is large and fierce looking, although he is extremely friendly to those who are brave enough to approach him. "These people who would usually keep their distance just came right up to Charlie and hugged him. Many people wanted to give him water or a treat. At one point Charlie was resting, and I turned away for a minute. When I turned around, this big burly guy was lying next to him, cuddling him. People definitely feel more at ease and let their guard down more with a dog than with a fellow human being, especially these police officers and firefighters who think they are supposed to be able to handle something like this."

Charlie took it all in stride, comforting those who needed it most, then returning eagerly to the task at hand when it was safe to return to the rubble.

Suzanne and Charlie continued to work at Ground Zero for several weeks until Suzanne learned she was pregnant. She and Charlie were immediately pulled from active duty. Suzanne was given a desk job, where she has been keeping busy sending thank you notes to the thousands of people and businesses who donated money, dog booties, dog food, and other essentials to the relief effort. Although Charlie is restless and obviously misses his job, he seems to understand that he has a new duty. "He's always been attached to me, but now he's all over me all the time," says Suzanne with a laugh. "At the station, we joke that the other dogs must be laughing at him. He's definitely a momma's boy. He used to like to lie in my lap, but now he can't do that anymore. So he'll get up on the couch and lie with his head on my stomach and one paw resting above my stomach and one below. He never lets me out of his sight."

One day Charlie and Suzanne will return to their jobs patrolling the streets, but for now, they are taking a much-deserved break. They, along with Suzanne's husband, Matt, a fellow police officer, are awaiting the newest addition to the family. Although Suzanne is Charlie's first love, she and Matt have no doubt that the Shepherd will show the same loyalty and protectiveness toward his new charge.

MAX

Bob Pintye of the Plumsted Township Police in New Jersey was in court the morning of September 11. When the second plane hit the Twin Towers, court was dismissed. Bob rushed home to pick up his 4-year-old search and rescue dog, Max. Bob intended to head to the police station to see what he could do to help, but by the time he got home, the station had already called—he was needed in New York.

Because the New Jersey Turnpike was closed to all but emergency vehicles headed to lower Manhattan, Bob was able to make it to Ground Zero in forty-five minutes. Several police officers met Bob as he drove up. Once they checked his ID and realized he was a police officer, they pulled him from the car, eager for the help they so desperately needed. Bob explained that he also needed his pouch that carried water, dog biscuits and some energy snacks for himself, and he needed to get his dog from the back.

By 1:30 P.M., Bob and Max were on the rubble.

"I don't even know where to begin," says Bob, trying to describe the devastation he encountered. "Here were two buildings over one hundred stories each, reduced to a 20-foot-high pile. There were bodies and body parts everywhere, but we weren't finding anyone alive."

Search and rescue dogs get their greatest reward from finding a living, breathing person who will respond gratefully to their enthusiastic licks. At the World Trade Center, there were no live finds to keep Max's spirits up. As they discovered victim after victim, Bob could see Max becoming visibly depressed. Max also seemed to be picking up on the somber demeanor of the firefighters.

"Ideally, I would have had a person hide in the rubble so Max could 'find' someone to keep his spirits up," says Bob. "But the situation was too difficult. No one could be spared from the search."

At one point, Bob stopped Max and started to play with him, petting him and talking enthusiastically to him to lift his spirits enough to go on. At first, he noticed a lot of suspicious looks from the firefighters, and a few asked how he could be acting so happy. When he explained what he was doing, many firefighters began to join in. Soon there was a line of firefighters taking off their gloves to pet Max. The more he was petted, the more pumped up Max became, and he was able to continue his job.

Bob and Max worked about twelve hours that first day, taking only brief rests before going back to searching the rubble. "Whenever the firefighters found a fire truck or an ambulance, they would call us over to search," says Bob. "These firefighters are an incredibly tight bunch of people. Many of them were searching for their fathers, sons, or brothers. But most of the trucks we found were crushed."

At one point, Bob took a moment to call his wife, Linda, on his cell phone. He told her he was standing next to Tower 7. Linda, who was watching the television coverage from home, located Tower 7 on the diagram being shown on the news. A moment after Bob hung up, Tower 7 collapsed.

"I felt my knees buckle," says Linda. "I was sure he was dead."

At the first sign of the crumbling tower, several firefighters threw Bob and Max into an alcove in the rubble and shielded them with their bodies to protect the team that was trying to save their relatives and friends. When the dust settled, Bob called Linda back to tell her he was okay.

Bob and Max returned to Ground Zero two more times, but were unable to locate anyone alive. By that time, dogs who were specially trained to search rubble and to search for cadavers were arriving from around the country. "Bob said he was okay after being there, but he didn't sleep right for a month afterwards," says Linda. Max, who has performed many tireless searches, was also affected by his experiences at the World Trade Center. "When he came home, he just lay down and wouldn't move," Bob says. "It took Max about a week to get over it. He usually likes to sleep outside, but for that week, he wanted to be inside with us. I would bring him in at night and just lie next to him on the floor, rubbing his ears and telling him what a good dog he is."

Max had been a search and rescue dog for about two years when the horror of September 11 hit. He has been called to service by five area townships to help find people lost in the woods, Alzheimer's patients who had wandered off, and fleeing crime suspects.

Max experienced his first civilian find when a three-year-old boy was missing at a local campground. Search dogs from the county had been looking for the boy for several hours when Max joined the team. Max alerted searchers to several abandoned cars and a play area, but they did not find the missing child. Later, Bob and Linda learned that the boy had earlier played in all the areas Max noted.

Linda asked the mother for a better scent object, one that would be saturated with the boy's scent. The mother handed over a hat the boy wore every day. Max stuck his muzzle in the hat and immediately took off toward yet another abandoned car. Max ran to the car, then ran away from it about 20 yards. Max, who tracks by air scent rather than trailing on the ground, then threw his nose up into the wind and raced back to the car, jumping and clawing on the door to get in.

Linda, who was standing next to the car, saw the little boy jump up on the seat before Max did. "The boy couldn't even talk yet, but I heard him say 'ding ding,' imitating the cow bell Max wears on his collar so we can find him when he's searching at night."

The boy had apparently become frightened by thunderstorms earlier in the day and had sought refuge in the car, curling up in a ball on the floor. Older children who were interviewed after the boy was found knew the car well from games of hide and seek and told police it was easy to get into but it was difficult to open the doors from the inside. The little boy had been missing for five hours when Max found him, and he was dehydrated from the heat and from crying. "It was a hot day in

August," says Linda. "He could have died in that car if Max hadn't found him."

Max seems to understand the difference between searching for a missing person and searching for a suspect. Bob believes Max picks up on his own demeanor and knows he is more relaxed when searching for a missing civilian. "When we're searching for a suspect, Max is on a 30-foot leash. There are a lot of woods in our area, and I'm always on the alert that a suspect could jump us from behind the bushes and trees. When we're searching for a civilian, Max is off-lead, and he can tell that I'm not in as high a state of alert."

Although Bob and Linda have no doubt that Max would defend them if needed, their gentle giant treats everyone as a friend until he learns otherwise. One day, he was trailing a robbery suspect. He found a discarded mask, outer clothing, and the money from the robbery. Across a mall parking lot, police were questioning a man who was sitting alone in his car in a corner of the lot. Suddenly, the police spied Max running full speed toward them.

"The police said he was running so fast they couldn't see any space between the ground and his belly," says Linda. Max ran straight past the officers and jumped into the car and onto the suspect's lap, showering his face with enthusiastic licks. "Max didn't realize this was a bad guy," says Bob. "All he knew was that he had been trailing the guy and had found a lost person."

After being identified by Max, the man immediately confessed to the crime.

Max surely will find many more missing persons in the years ahead. But it is doubtful that he will ever take part in a search as meaningful, and as heartbreaking, as the search at Ground Zero.

TIKVA

We've all seen the stories of the courageous search and rescue dogs called to duty following the devastating attack on the World Trade Center. Less public were the deeds of a team of therapy dogs who traveled from Oregon to give comfort to those at the scene.

Cindy Ehlers is founder of HOPE AAA/AAT (Helping Overcome Problems Everywhere: Animal Assisted Activities/Animal Assisted Therapy) and HOPE AACR (Animal Assisted Crisis Response). She first became involved in therapy work in 1997 with her Keeshond, Bear, who showed amazing empathy to people in emotional turmoil. When Cindy obtained her second Keeshond, Tikva, she hoped her new dog would pick up on Bear's sensitivity. In April 2001, Tikva officially became a Delta Society Therapy Dog.

Cindy explains that HOPE offers three different levels of therapy: animal assisted activities (AAA), in which canine/handler teams visit schools, nursing homes, and hospitals; animal assisted therapy (AAT), in which dogs participate in documented visits and are actually part of a patient's treatment plan with a directed goal in mind (such as having a stroke victim brush the dog's fur with his left hand to increase mobility); and animal assisted crisis response (AACR), in which animals assist mental health counselors in a crisis situation. Cindy says AACR takes therapy to a much higher level, since dogs must be stable in a crisis situation and must be familiar with people in emotional trauma.

As the events of September 11 unfolded, Cindy's brother, a firefighter for Los Angeles County in California, was called to the scene. Once there, he saw the toll the devastation was taking on the rescue workers and felt his sister and her dog could offer much needed comfort. He spoke with a firefighter chaplain, who alerted the Red Cross, and, as a result, Cindy and Tikva, along with three other canine/handler teams from HOPE, made the journey to New York. They arrived on September 21, and for two weeks, they did their best to ease the emotional pain borne by the recovery workers and the victims' families.

Cindy and Tikva arrived at the mobile veterinary unit that had been set up for the search and rescue dogs. Tikva had a thorough check-up to be sure she was ready for the task at hand. Tikva was outfitted with special booties to protect her feet, then she and Cindy traveled to the Red Cross station set up in a school near the World Trade Center site. They met with a mental health counselor, then the team set out for Ground Zero. They walked the entire site, stopping to talk to rescue workers and trying to get them to share their experiences and somehow lighten their emotional burden. It took approximately four hours to get around the entire site. The mental health counselor accompanying Cindy and Tikva had never worked with a therapy dog before, and she was amazed at the difference the Keeshond made. Grim-faced rescue workers who refused to talk about their feelings would speak to Tikva. The counselor commented that Tikva could accomplish more in a few minutes than she could accomplish in several hours.

Once their tour of the site was completed, Cindy and Tikva returned to the Red Cross cafeteria, where they took a two-hour break and grabbed a bite to eat. Although they were officially on break, Cindy says Tikva was still on the job. The rescue workers also stopped at the Red Cross station for food, and Cindy quickly realized that they gained tremendous comfort from offering the dogs something to eat. "It was an emotional release to feed and pet the dogs at the cafeteria," says Cindy. "A biological change takes place when we touch. While some people find it difficult to touch another person in a time of crisis, it's okay to touch a dog. Petting a dog actually lowers blood pressure. When someone's blood pressure goes down, they relax, and once they relax, they begin to talk."

In general, Cindy gives Tikva free reign to choose whom she feels most needs comfort. The Keeshond has a specific manner of approaching in a gentle, nonthreatening way those who are distraught. "First, she goes over and touches her nose to their knee," says Cindy. "If they look at her, she raises a paw in a type of wave. If they respond, she'll put her paws on their lap. If they lean forward, she puts her face close to them, and if they respond to that, she puts her paws on their shoulders in a hug."

Cindy recalls one firefighter who seemed particularly withdrawn. She gently placed Tikva in his lap, and he immediately began petting her. Tikva nuzzled her head into his arm, and he began to speak softly, so only the dog could hear. When Tikva finally got down and she and

Cindy started to walk away, the man thanked her and asked if they could come visit him again.

Tikva also helped console the families of victims of the attacks. Ferry boats were shuttling family members from Pier 94 to Ground Zero to enable them to put closure on the loss of their loved ones. Mayor Giuliani requested that the dogs be stationed on the boats. Cindy says the emotions on those trips were different from those experienced with the rescue workers. "The families welcomed the dogs in a more obvious way. Once they had interacted with the dogs, many of them didn't want to let the dogs out of their sight."

One woman who had lost her husband saw Tikva and immediately reached out and hugged her and began crying. Another woman, who had flown in from Russia after the death of her son at the World Trade Center, grabbed Tikva's cheeks and started speaking to her in Russian. Tikva responded by licking away her tears.

Although all four dogs from HOPE showed tremendous empathy to the workers and families, one dog found it too much to bear. While at the site, a German Shepherd named Uno began to alert to something in the ground in typical search and rescue dog fashion and became depressed. Eventually, he was moved to the family assistance center. "There was something about that particular spot at Ground Zero," says Cindy. "All the dogs became very solemn in the spot where Uno alerted. It was an area that had been paved over to allow tractors into the site, so rescue workers weren't looking for bodies there, they were looking in the area that was called 'the pit'. This particular area was where the underground mall had been located, right near the Marriott Hotel. I believe a lot of souls may have perished there, and that is what the dogs were reacting to."

When the time came for all the teams to return home, their presence was sorely missed at Ground Zero. Many rescue workers asked where the "comfort dogs" had gone and when would they be back. One firefighter confessed, "Seeing those dogs was the only thing that got me through the day."

LOUISE

Louise the Bearded Collie is neither a search and rescue dog nor a trained therapy dog. Yet, she managed to push aside her own terror on September 11 and found a way to comfort others.

On September 11, Louise was riding through lower Manhattan in the car with her owners, Abigail and Tony McGrath. The McGraths suddenly noticed people congregating and looking up at the skyline. "When we got to the North Bridge, people under the bridge were pointing up like in a bad Godzilla movie," recalls Abigail.

Suddenly, debris began to rain down on the highway, and something heavy struck the McGrath's car. They quickly pulled off onto a side street to survey the damage and got their first glimpse of the damaged World Trade Center. Smoke billowed from the gaping hole in the building's side and papers flew through the air. Abigail grabbed for her video camera and was checking the battery when Louise made it clear she needed to be walked. As they took a brief walk to let Louise relieve herself, Abigail noticed her cell phone wasn't working. Her stomach churned as she took in the scene; still, she could not imagine the magnitude of what was happening. When they got back to the car, Abigail saw flames shooting from the building. She hurriedly pushed Louise into the car, then she heard the deafening sound of a jet as the second terrorist plane headed toward Tower Two. Someone shouted to get down. Abigail dropped to the ground and rolled under her car, along with Tony and a stranger who had been standing next to them.

They remained there for a long time, listening to the deafening explosions. When they finally felt it was safe to get up, they realized that Louise was gone. Abigail was heartsick. As Abigail and Tony slowly drove toward Battery Park, they asked everyone they met with a dog to keep an eye out for the Beardie. When they reached the park, Abigail saw the fear in the police officers' eyes.

Abigail will never forget what happened next. "Suddenly, with no warning, the first building fell. It was like an enormous tumbleweed billowing through a cavern. There was smoke and ash everywhere."

The police told everyone to get out of their cars and run to the park. There, throngs of people tried to make their way through the choking, acrid smoke. Although they could barely see where they were going, Abigail and Tony could make out the water line and began to walk north. They passed a laundry truck where the driver was handing out towels; an act of kindness they will never forget. Abigail noticed a young woman wailing while a stranger tried to comfort her and urged her to drink some water. The woman responded, "It's not me; my mother works in the World Trade Center." Abigail realized that people were dying.

Suddenly, the second tower fell with the same deafening sound as the first. Abigail and Tony pressed on, finally splitting up so that Tony could retrieve the car and Abigail could walk home in case Louise had found her way back. As Abigail walked in the door of their home, the phone was ringing. It was Heather Crawford calling from the Liberty Park Water Taxi, which had been turned into a rescue barge. She had Louise. Abigail listened as Heather described how her boyfriend, Captain Chuck Ruch, had rescued Louise and what had happened to the dog in the past several hours.

After Louise escaped from the car, she ran toward Ground Zero, not realizing the danger in front of her. Chuck saw where she was headed and stepped on her leash to stop her. He held her back and waited, expecting Louise's owners to show up any minute. After a while, Chuck decided to take Louise with him to the Hudson River where they could catch a Water Taxi. Suddenly, he looked up and saw an enormous cloud of thick, gray smoke and large chunks of debris rumbling toward him faster than he could possibly run. He and Louise managed to run onto the pier and Chuck leaped onto a yacht. When Louise refused to jump after him, he returned to the pier, picked up the 55-pound dog and jumped back onto the yacht. He smashed the etched glass window on the door of the boat with his hand and climbed into the boat, pulling Louise in behind him. He

then tacked a tablecloth over the open doorway and settled down with Louise, believing they were going to die

The cloud that soon surrounded the boat was too
thick for light to penetrate, and Chuck and Louise were
cloaked in darkness. After some time, however, the cloud
began to dissipate. Chuck looked out and found a police
boat beside the yacht. When Chuck told the police he was
a ship captain, they asked him to join them ferrying
people, and bodies, back and forth between Manhattan
and Liberty State Park in New Jersey. He quickly agreed,
and insisted that Louise accompany him.

So Louise joined Chuck on his numerous journeys
across the water aboard a NYPD harbor patrol boat. This
dog, who had been so filled with terror that she had left the
safety of her owners' car, now calmed perfect strangers.
When the injured on stretchers saw her, they managed to
smile. When terrified children covered with ash met the
Beardie, they stopped crying.

After riding back and forth for several trips, Louise
got off at Liberty State Park. She made her way through
the endless stretchers, padding from patient to patient
giving licks and offering soft fur to dry their tears. She
also offered comfort to the workers, leaning against them
as they gave her a hug and a pat that nourished their soul.
Louise stayed on the job for several days until Abigail
could retrieve her. She nursed the wounded for long peri-
ods of time, then returned with her rescuer and Heather
to their boat for some much-needed rest.

When Abigail was finally reunited with her dog, she
couldn't believe the impact Louise had made. Everyone at
the marina knew her, and the workers asked if she could

possibly stay a few more days. Although Abigail knew Louise had helped many, she was concerned for the dog's well-being and decided to bring her home.

What makes Louise's story even more remarkable is that the Bearded Collie had been abandoned earlier in her life, and had only been living in a stable, loving home with the McGraths for nine months when the World Trade Center was hit. Still, she managed to bring love to those who needed it most during a time of indescribable horror.

Abigail is in the process of writing a children's book based on Louise. "The book is about a dog who is rejected as a failure but finds one thing she can do—make people happy."

SIRIUS

Bomb-detection dog Sirius, a yellow Labrador Retriever, is believed to be the only canine to die in the attack on the World Trade Center. Port Authority Police Officer David Lim and four-year-old Sirius had worked as partners since March 2000, searching commercial vehicles entering the World Trade Center. In their time together, they helped clear the way for visits by dignitaries such as then-President Bill Clinton, Minnesota Governor Jesse Ventura, and Palestinian leader Yasser Arafat.

On the morning of September 11, David left Sirius in his Port Authority kennel in the basement of Tower Two to help in Tower One, which had just been hit. David promised his dog he would be back soon, never imagining that the same unspeakable horror would soon befall the second tower. When Tower Two was hit and David received the call to evacuate, he stopped on the fifth floor of Tower One to help carry a woman down to safety. They had reached the fourth floor when the building suddenly collapsed on top of them. Miraculously, David was rescued five hours later with just a mild concussion.

Doctors refused to allow David to search for Sirius in the rubble of Ground Zero due to the emotional toll it would take on him. Still, he kept abreast of the rescue efforts, hoping his partner would be found. Finally, on January 24, 2002, Sirius's remains were recovered, and David was called to the scene. All work at the site was stopped, and Sirius was carried out with full honors, including an American flag covering him and a salute by the waiting police officers and firefighters. David found consolation in the fact that the kennel appeared to have collapsed, killing Sirius instantly.

"I've been waiting to find him," newspapers reported David saying. "I fulfilled my promise to him because I came back, and I took him home."

There were countless other dogs who showed their compassion in the face of the devastating events of September 11.

- Bear the Golden Retriever saved three of the five survivors found in the first twenty-four hours after the attack on the World Trade Center. Since the attack, Bear has had his portrait painted and has been saluted by the bagpipers of the Scots Guards. As of this printing, the town of Westport, Connecticut, was considering erecting a statue of Bear crawling through the wreckage to honor the Golden.

• Appollo, a nine-year-old German Shepherd, was awarded the American Kennel Club's 2001 Award for Canine Excellence (ACE) in the Law Enforcement Category. Appollo, a member of the New York Police Department's K-9 Unit, is trained for gun recovery, urban search and rescue, and cadaver search. In addition to his work fighting crime, Appollo is certified by the Federal Emergency Management Association for search and rescue work. He has answered the call of duty at numerous disasters, including the Dominican Republic in the wake of Hurricane George and various building collapses around New York City. On the day the AKC was to announce its ACE recipients, September 11, 2001, the World Trade Center was attacked, and Appollo reported once more for duty. While walking on the hot debris, the ground suddenly gave out beneath Appollo's feet and flames shot up from the hole where he had disappeared. When his handler, Peter Davis, pulled him out and brushed off the glowing embers, Appollo rushed back to work.

Appollo continued to search the World Trade Center site every day until the beginning of January 2002; then he went on a rotating schedule of two to three days a week with the other search dogs. Appollo has received even more awards based on his latest heroic actions. Along with many of his K-9 comrades, Appollo was honored for his bravery at the 2002

Westminster Dog Show in New York City. He and the other rescue dogs at the World Trade Center and the Pentagon also received Britain's animal version of the Victoria Cross, the Dickin Medal. The awarding of this medal was instituted in 1943 to recognize animals displaying "conspicuous gallantry and devotion to duty" while serving with the Armed Forces and civil defense units during World War II and its aftermath. This is the first time the Dickin Medal has been awarded for activities outside of war.

- Two yellow Labrador Retriever guide dogs, Roselle and Salty, led their owners to safety down the stairway of the World Trade Center minutes before the towers collapsed. Michael Hingson was preparing for a meeting on the seventy-eighth floor of the north tower when it was hit. Roselle quickly helped him locate the stairs, and they began the long trip down. After about an hour, they finally reached street level and managed to escape the area before the building collapsed. Upon the collapse of the second tower, Roselle helped lead a stranger to safety after the woman was blinded by debris in her eyes. Omar Rivera and Salty were on the seventy-first floor and made the same dangerous trek down the smoky, crowded stairway. Like Appollo, both dogs were recognized with a number of awards, including Britain's Dickin Medal.

- Servus, a Belgian Malinois, and his handler, Chris Christensen, traveled from their home in Missouri to help the recovery efforts. While searching Ground

Zero, Servus fell 20 feet into a pile of debris. The dust and concrete ash filled his nostrils, preventing him from breathing. A nurse at the scene quickly administered IV fluids and a firefighter suctioned his airwaves. He began to convulse and was rushed to a local veterinary hospital, where the veterinarians stabilized him. After observing him for several hours, the vets released Servus, and he and Chris returned to the site. Chris ordered Servus to stay in the car while he rejoined the search, but the dog refused. So the two worked through the night until Servus fell again and once more began to convulse. This time, after Servus was treated, Chris pulled him off duty and set off on the long drive home.

CHAPTER 5

CANINE MEDICS

Some dogs show an uncanny sensitivity to their owners' health. From dogs who warn diabetic companions when their blood sugar is too low to canines who predict impending epileptic seizures, many dogs are effective nurses to their human best friends.

MICHELANGELO

Suzanne of Chicago, Illinois, knows the tremendous impact a service dog can have on one's life. Due to a medical condition, she has mobility problems, suffers from a lack of balance, and uses a walker or cane to get around. Suzanne also has epilepsy. Her Standard Poodle, Bonar, is trained for mobility assistance, retrieval work, and bracing. Suzanne knew she would be lost without a service dog, but she never dreamed that two service dogs would be better than one.

Michelangelo came into Suzanne's life in April 2001. Suzanne and her husband, Randy, were attending a "pet swap" at a local fairground one weekend when they wandered over to a pen that held five fluffy Shih Tzu/Poodle mix puppies. Suzanne asked her husband to hand her one puppy who caught her eye. As she cradled the puppy in her arms, a woman came over and asked the puppies' breeder how much she wanted for all of the dogs in the pen except the puppy Suzanne held, assuming Suzanne was going to purchase the pup. Suzanne did not need another dog—at the time she was waiting for Bonar to finish his service dog training. She was about to tell the woman this, when the woman explained that she wanted the pups strictly for breeding purposes. Suzanne knew this likely meant the puppies would be permanently caged and never receive the attention they deserved. Suzanne wrote a check for the puppy she was holding, all the while telling herself that she would find a home for the puppy with people who would love him and make him a part of their family. Still, she and her husband stopped at the local pet supply store on the way home to pick up a crate and a few toys, just in case they couldn't place the puppy right away.

At first, Suzanne refused to name the new dog. She called him Puppy and tried not to get too attached to the beautiful little ball of fluff. Puppy, however, seemed to have other plans. He affixed himself to Suzanne and worked to win her over by learning several commands and becoming housetrained within days. On Monday, Suzanne took the puppy to the veterinarian to be checked over and to receive his shots. The vet asked for his name, and Suzanne told him, "Well, we don't know if we're going to keep him, but I think we'll call him Michael Anthony."

The vet laughed and suggested Michelangelo. Suzanne couldn't resist, and Puppy was renamed. Suzanne still resisted the idea of keeping Michelangelo, until the day he saved her life.

Suzanne was descending the hardwood stairs in her home, using the wall and railing for balance. Randy was behind her carrying Michelangelo. As they went down the stairs, the little dog began to squirm and tap Suzanne on the shoulder. She looked up and told Randy to hold onto the dog, but he kept squirming. Randy said the puppy seemed to want to be with her and handed him over. Suzanne reached up to take the puppy, then turned to continue back down the stairs. Suddenly Suzanne felt as if the floor was spinning, and she began to pitch forward. She yelled to Randy to take Michelangelo, then, once the puppy was safe, she dropped to the stairs and crawled up to the bedroom. She knew she didn't have much time until an epileptic seizure hit. She tried to crawl to the bed, but the seizure hit before she could make it.

When Suzanne came out of the seizure, Michelangelo jumped on her chest, and began kissing her face. Suzanne knew at that moment that she could end her search for a family for Michelangelo—he had already found one.

Suzanne says, "Had Michelangelo not alerted me by tapping my shoulder, I would have taken the next step and fallen the rest of the way down head first, possibly breaking my back or neck. There was no doubt that he saved me from what could have been a fatal fall."

Since that day, Michelangelo has alerted Suzanne to other seizures and is learning to work in tandem with Bonar as a service dog team. Although Suzanne has been seizure-free since July 2001, she is continuing with Michelangelo's training just in case.

"At first, Bonar wasn't sure that he wanted to share his 'mother' with another working dog," says Suzanne. Gradually, however, Bonar learned to step back when Michelangelo alerted, and then to be ready to help Suzanne to a chair or bed. Michelangelo is now officially listed as a service dog in training, while Bonar is a certi- fied service dog.

"After a time, Bonar and Mikey became brothers," says Suzanne. "They now will kiss each other, with Mikey initiating the cuddle session. Without them, I would be lost."

NICK

Joni Kay Muir of Stevensville, Montana, tells of a very special dog who entered her life twice—and saved it the second time.

Joni is involved with Greyhound rescue, helping to find new homes for dogs who have retired from racing. One day a friend called to tell Joni about two male Grey- hounds whose family was being forced to give them up due to a life crisis. As Joni's friend described the dogs, she realized she knew one of them; she had pulled him from the track and placed him nine years before.

Joni says, "I have always believed a rescue person, like a good breeder, is responsible for the dogs they place."

Joni called the dog's owner and asked if she would be willing to place the dogs in separate homes. The woman hesitated and then explained that she was worried the older dog wouldn't be able to find a suitable home. She was surprised when Joni explained that she wanted only the older dog. Joni explained her connection to the Greyhound, and the woman agreed to let her meet Nick.

Joni's husband, Darrin, needed a little more convincing. He didn't understand why they needed to add another dog to their existing pack of six. Joni assured him that Nick probably wouldn't be with them very long, since he was eleven years old and both of their previous Greyhounds had died during their eleventh year. He finally consented and Nick came home.

Nick had some neck and back problems that had gone untreated for years. A local veterinarian tried acupuncture and chiropractic adjustments, and Joni changed Nick's diet and began using massage on the affected areas. The change in Nick was dramatic. When Nick first came to live with Joni, it was difficult for him to bend his neck. If he moved suddenly, he would often cry out in pain. His fastest movement was a lumbering side-to-side trot that appeared painful. With the new treatments, Nick could bend, run full speed, and even spin in circles. During the treatments, Joni and Nick began to bond. But it wasn't until months later that she realized the depth of this bond.

The autumn after she brought Nick home, Joni became sick. She had difficulty catching her breath and her lungs hurt. It was a lingering problem that wore her down a little at a time. It was so gradual that she could almost ignore it.

One day, as she was getting ready to leave for work, Nick began to act up. Joni wasn't feeling well but was pushing on with the day. Nick became very vocal, barking louder and more frantically until spit was flying and he was near hysteria. Joni couldn't imagine what was wrong with him. She called in late for work and spent a few minutes trying to calm him down. Each time he seemed to be settling down, Joni tried to leave, but Nick would demand that she return. Finally, Joni called the office to say she would be taking a sick day. Since she was staying home, Joni made an afternoon doctor's appointment and spent the day sleeping. Nick stayed nearby, keeping an eye on her. Strangely, when Joni got up to go to her appointment, Nick was perfectly content to let her leave the house.

Joni was shocked when a chest x-ray showed that her heart was extremely enlarged. An emergency echocardiogram was scheduled for the next day. After the echocardiogram and consultation with a cardiologist, Joni learned that she had a severe case of pericarditis, or fluid in the sack surrounding the heart. Joni was started on several medications to help diminish the fluid, and she was ordered to rest. After a few days, she started to rally, but then her condition deteriorated again. During these days, Nick stayed where he could see Joni at all times.

One Friday, Joni didn't feel well when she got up, but she assured her husband that she would be fine once the medication kicked in. When Darrin left for work, Nick seemed to cling closer than ever. Over the next couple of hours, Joni's condition became more severe. Any movement sent her into fits of wheezing and fighting for air. By evening, he was drenched in sweat and couldn't find a comfortable position. Although the rest of Joni's dogs were crated during the night, Nick was allowed run of the house. Nick stood beside Joni's bed, watching his owner writhing in pain. Joni realized she was in serious trouble. She tried to get up to get to a phone, but it was a struggle. Nick clung to her side, offering his back for balance. He crowded Joni against the wall so that she could lean on it. When she felt as if she were going to pass out, he touched her skin with his cold nose and encouraged her to keep going. The eight or so feet to the phone seemed like a mile, but Nick took every step with Joni, offering not only emotional support, but also his body if she needed it. Finally, Joni reached the phone and called for help. When her sister arrived, Nick barked and ran to the door. He returned to Joni's side and stayed with her as her sister helped her to the car.

Joni was hospitalized and had an emergency tap done on her heart. Darrin reported that during the time she was hospitalized, Nick watched the door for his mistress's return. At night, he stood at the door and whined, sometimes for more than an hour. Joni wished their was some way to get a message to her precious dog that she was going to recover and return to him soon.

Joni was released on Christmas Eve. Although all her dogs reacted to her homecoming, with some sniffing her from head to toe as if they understood something had been wrong, none reacted quite like Nick, who was overjoyed at her return. "He followed my every move, play bowing at every turn and whining in delight. He refused to go outside unless I accompanied him." That evening,

Joni realized what an important role Nick had played in helping her through the crisis. She sat on the couch watching her St. Nick in the light of the Christmas tree, tears of gratitude flowing down her face.

"I feel so blessed to share my life with Nick," says Joni. "I am not sure God could have made a more perfect soul. I am humbled when I realize that this dog who only came here to spend his last days has given me everything he has. I never expected to bond with him in this way—he was only temporary. Little did I know when I signed that adoption paper from Greyhound Pets of America that I was adopting an angel."

SUZIE Q

Carol Grant's Aunt Eleanor lost her husband several years ago. They had been very close, and she had difficulty adjusting to living alone. About two years after her husband's death, Eleanor visited Carol and fell in love with her Pomeranian, Smokey. Carol and her husband decided a puppy might ease Eleanor's loneliness. Eleanor immediately fell in love with the tiny dog and named her Suzie Q.

About a year after coming to live with Eleanor, Suzie Q awakened her owner with desperate staccato barks. Focusing on the dog, Eleanor couldn't figure out what was wrong. She touched her hand to her brow and suddenly realized she was sweating profusely. Eleanor, a diabetic, immediately checked her sugar level and discovered it was dangerously low. She quickly took her medicine and turned to Suzie Q who sat down and "smiled" at her owner.

"Apparently Suzie Q sensed something was wrong and decided to awaken Aunt Eleanor," says Carol. "If she had not done this, we might have lost our aunt."

TILLA

Donna Lindsay of Eagle River, Alaska, has a Sheltie, Tilla, who helps her control her rare genetic disorder called Andersen's Syndrome, a type of periodic paralysis. Donna experiences potassium losses that cause temporary muscle weakness, total paralysis, or even cardiac complications that could lead to cardiac arrest. Tilla senses when Donna's potassium is getting low, and in the middle of the night, she lets Donna know when she needs to take more potassium. She does this by getting up on the bed, sharing Donna's pillow, and being more "clingy" than usual. She keeps pestering her owner until Donna takes her medicine, after which Tilla resumes her regular post on the hope chest at the foot of the bed.

"I know that if Tilla is on the bed, there is a reason for it. She can sense the attack at least a half hour before it starts," says Donna.

Tilla's sensitivity also makes her particularly perceptive of people's emotions; even people she doesn't know very well.

"Tilla is a typically reserved Sheltie," says Donna. "She's not in the least bit shy, but when people she doesn't know well come over to the house, she holds back. She's somewhat slow to make friends. But if someone is upset about anything, even a stranger, she will jump up on the sofa next to them, offer them a paw, tilt her head this way and that, and look very concerned. She's what I call a Guardian Sheltie. She takes care of people's emotional needs."

CAESAR

When Barb Williams of Canastota, New York, left for college, she was reluctant to leave her Lab cross, Caesar, behind. She knew her parents would take good care of him, however, so she embarked on her four-year adventure, seeing her dog when she returned home for holidays and summer vacations. Although Caesar was always happy to see her, each time she came home, she noticed that he seemed increasingly attached to her parents. After graduation, Barb decided to move out of her childhood home and strike out on her own. By this time, Caesar seemed more her parents' dog than hers, so she made the difficult decision to leave him behind. Little did she know that decision would save her mother's life.

On New Year's Eve, 1997, Barb's mother, Margaret Kurak, was home alone with just Caesar for company. While climbing the stairs from the basement, she stumbled and fell down the steps, severely injuring herself. Caesar attempted to rush to his owner's aid, but at the top of the stairs, he skidded to a stop. He had been trained to never go down the cellar steps. Faced with this imaginary barrier, Caesar did the one thing he could to help his owner— he let out an anguished bark. He continued to bark for the next four hours, while she lay at the bottom of the stairs trying to console him, letting him know that she was okay.

She passed the time by talking to Caesar and trying to re-assure him.

When Barb's father returned home, he discovered Margaret and called an ambulance. Margaret was rushed to the hospital where she was diagnosed with a fractured skull, a broken arm, and bruising on the front and back of her brain. She also had a gash in her scalp that required twenty-two stitches, and she had lost a lot of blood. The attending doctors were amazed that she had not slipped into a coma. When they heard that Caesar kept her talking during those four long hours, they knew that was the only reason she had remained lucid.

That night in the neurological unit, the nurses heard Margaret calling out in her sleep to her dog, saying, "Caesar, it's okay, Mommy is just lying down."

Margaret recovered, but she never forgot the heroic actions of her daughter's dog, who had truly become her own. One night, several years later, Caesar walked into Margaret's bedroom, laid down next to the bed, and died peacefully in his sleep, right by his mistress' side.

ENDAL

Endal, a four-year-old Labrador Retriever, has become something of a celebrity in his native England. Among his many honors, Endal has been dubbed Britain's most intelligent animal and Dog of the Millennium.

Endal is a service dog partner to Gulf War veteran Allen Parton, who is confined to a wheelchair due to injuries sustained in a car crash during his military service.

As a result of the accident, Allen was left with several disabilities.

Endal and Allen were united when Allen's wife was training dogs for Canine Partners for Independence, which teaches dogs to help their disabled owners by navigating all types of everyday challenges—from pushing elevator buttons to taking laundry out of the washing machine. One day, Allen accompanied his wife to a program event and sat in a corner, watching but remaining apart from the action. By this time, Allen had retreated from most human contact and would either ignore people who tried to speak with him or would treat them rudely so they would leave him alone. On the other side of the room, Endal was also experiencing problems. The Lab seemed destined to fail the training program due to a disability of his own—intermittent OCD, or osteochondritis dissecans, a painful disorder of immature bones. When Endal and Allen were introduced to each other, there was an immediate connection. The director of the program watched the positive effect the two seemed to be having on each other. She decided to give Endal a chance and sent him home with Allen for a trial period. The two became instant friends, and as Endal's condition cleared up, he blossomed in his role as a service dog.

Endal first attracted national attention when he took over for Allen at an ATM machine, jumping up to retrieve the money, card, and receipt without being asked. A television crew heard about the feat and decided to try to catch Endal on film. The first time Allen handed him the ATM card, Endal placed it in the correct slot, and a canine celebrity was born.

Endal wasn't fully trained when he left the Canine Partners' program, and Allen stresses that most of what Endal does is self-taught. One of Allen's disabilities is memory loss. Often, he will meet someone on the street whom he has known for years, yet he can't remember the person. Endal has made these encounters less stressful.

"If someone asks, 'How is Endal today?' I know we're acquaintances."

Allen also suffers "word blindness," where he can't recall the word for something he needs. One day, Allen was searching for his wheelchair gloves but couldn't express what he wanted. Finally, he touched his hand in frustration. Endal immediately retrieved his gloves. Allen realized that Endal could be taught sign language, and Endal now has a vast vocabulary of hand signals that Allen uses when words fail him. This ability helped Endal win the title of "Britain's most intelligent animal" from the BBC after a worldwide search.

Endal again proved his amazing problem-solving ability and heroism during the renowned Crufts dog show in spring 2001. Allen and Endal had just arrived at Crufts, where they had been invited to demonstrate the abilities of service dogs, when a car suddenly came bearing down at them in reverse. Allen managed to shove Endal out of the way, but had no time to escape himself, and the vehicle crashed into his wheelchair, knocking him to the ground.

Endal sprang to action to help his injured owner. He rolled Allen from his back to the recovery position on his side, then retrieved the cell phone that was knocked from Allen's lap. He tapped the phone lightly against Allen's face, forcing him to focus and take it. Then he grabbed his dog blanket from under the wheelchair and covered his owner to keep him warm. By this time, Allen had recovered enough to ask his dog to get help. Endal ran to the hotel doors, barking, then ran back to his owner. Endal continued sounding the alarm until several people emerged from the hotel to help.

When an ambulance arrived to transport Allen to the hospital, Endal refused to leave his side. The ambulance crew allowed the dog to ride along, even lowering the stretcher support so Endal could keep a watchful eye on his partner.

Once at the hospital, Endal remained next to Allen while he was treated for grazes and bruising on his left side, hip, upper leg, and right elbow. The following day, Endal was examined by the Kennel Club's vets back at Crufts and found to be injury-free. Although a little shaken, Allen and Endal still put on their demonstration, which had taken on an extra dimension in light of the previous day's events.

On the final day of the show, Endal was presented with the Gold Kennel Club Good Citizen Award, which awards dogs for an obedient working relationship with their owners. He is believed to be the first assistance dog to ever receive the honor.

Endal and Allen have appeared on TV numerous times, demonstrating the role that assistance dogs play in the lives of their owners. Television crews from around the world have filmed him. He also has attracted quite a following—at Crufts he was recognized and sought out by people from numerous countries, and he currently receives about three hundred e-mails a week from people around the world.

Allen says Endal has helped him in more ways than even being an assistance dog would imply. "Three and a half years ago I couldn't talk, read, or write and I had lost all emotion. Endal brought me back to life. I wouldn't still be married if it wasn't for him, I wouldn't be with my children, and I would still be in care, thought of as brain dead."

Above and beyond his incredible duties as Allen's helper, Endal has proven to be a loyal, loving companion. Allen says of his canine partner and friend: "There is a biblical misconception that guardian angels only have two legs—mine has four."

HARVEY

Support Dogs of Sheffield, England, submitted the following story of Gillian and Harvey. Gillian has faced more obstacles in her life than most people could bear, but she found the strength to go on through the love of a little black dog.

Gillian developed epilepsy at age three as the result of a high fever and convulsions suffered at nine months of age. A series of different drug therapies failed to help her, and she became hyperactive and aggressive toward her younger brother. Her family moved from England to Zambia in search of a less stressful life. Gillian's health didn't improve, and she and her parents continued to fly back and forth to England hoping for a breakthrough in her treatment.

When Gillian reached her teens, her family hoped she would outgrow her epilepsy, but she continued to have partial seizures. She enrolled in college as a beauty therapist, and when no one would employ her due to her epilepsy, her parents helped her start her own business. Several years later, she married and moved to South Africa in hopes of finding a doctor who could control her epilepsy. Gillian visited many neurologists in search of a cure and even tried homeopathic medicine. This turned out to be a dangerous decision; Gillian lapsed into a coma and was not expected to live. Somehow, she found the strength to pull herself back to her family. Gillian's attacks continued to occur randomly and without warning. Four years after giving birth to a daughter, Gillian's health began to deteriorate and her seizures occurred more frequently. Tests revealed that Gillian also had lupus, an incurable blood disease. Her liver was almost destroyed, she had very few red blood cells left, and her immune system was severely weakened. Gillian's parents came to South Africa to help look after their daughter.

In 1996, Gillian's aunt sent her a letter from England telling her about a program she had seen on television that showed how dogs can help people with uncontrolled epilepsy. Gillian wrote to Support Dogs but was told that since she was living in South Africa, she was too far away to be considered for a dog. By that time, Gillian was constantly in and out of the hospital and didn't know if she would survive from one day to the next. Tragically, Gillian's husband committed suicide. Shortly after that, Gillian's mother was diagnosed with breast cancer. Gillian and her parents decided to return to England to be close to the rest of their family during this difficult time.

Once back in England, Gillian reapplied to Support Dogs and was told she might be a suitable candidate. She had always loved dogs and had been heartbroken when she had to leave her three dogs behind in South Africa.

Gillian says, "I was beginning to feel that I might be closer to that light at the end of the tunnel. My doctor's reaction when I told her the news was, 'Try anything.' I think she had given up on medications to control my epilepsy. I was taking nineteen tablets every day and still having countless attacks."

In February 2000, Gillian received a phone call from Paula, a Support Dogs trainer, who told her they had a little black dog that might be suitable for her. Gillian let herself feel the hope that had been eluding her for years. Paula told her the dog's name was Harvey and that she would bring a video of him.

"I really didn't need to see the video because I had already decided that Harvey would be mine," recalls Gillian. "A few weeks later, my father and I went up to Sheffield to meet him. He was adorable, and we bonded right away."

For two weeks, Gillian and her father traveled to Sheffield for Gillian and Harvey's training during the week, then returned home to Surrey on Friday. Harvey spent the weekends with a woman who had been socializing him for Support Dogs before his official training began. Gillian and Harvey bonded so quickly that Gillian's seizures were already occurring less often. For the third week of training, Harvey was allowed to stay with Gillian in her motel.

Harvey was taught to sense when Gillian became stressed or a seizure was coming. He learned specific behaviors to signal an attack. If Gillian was sitting down, he would sit very still and look at her in a peculiar way. If they went out for a walk, he would whimper.

"My seizure frequency was already much reduced, and I knew that Harvey would warn me if I wasn't feeling well," says Gillian. "This gave me the confidence to do things knowing that I wouldn't hurt myself."

Harvey soon learned that when he wears his red training jacket he is working. He is trained to walk at Gillian's pace, ignore food or anything else enticing on the street, be polite to children and adults, and always sit at the curb before crossing the street. Gillian carries identification and explains what type of assistance dog Harvey is to shopkeepers and pedestrians

"People soon began to recognize Harvey," says Gillian. "He is loved and respected by everyone. He has given me the confidence to go out on my own. I know that people understand Harvey's role and my epilepsy. I often heard people talking about Harvey, or 'that little dog in the red coat.' My seizure frequency decreased even more. The only seizures I get now are either from stress or lupus flares."

After nine months of training, Harvey qualified as a fully registered Seizure Alert Dog and earned his prestigious yellow jacket. Harvey continues to educate people about service dogs and demonstrate the incredible bond between an assistance dog and his owner.

Although Gillian's epileptic seizures have been drastically reduced, Harvey is still an important alarm system for her. In 2001, Gillian was diagnosed with malignant melanoma, a form of skin cancer. Treatment required surgery and general anesthesia. The surgeon had heard about Harvey and was so impressed with the dog's abilities that he asked if Gillian would like to have Harvey in the operating room so he could warn the staff if she were going to have a seizure. The doctor was concerned that the stress of the operation combined with Gillian's lupus might trigger an attack, but Gillian says having Harvey by her side kept her feeling strong and positive.

In March 2001, Harvey was nominated for the Golden Bonio award, which goes to the United Kingdom's Dog of the Year. Harvey was chosen one of ten finalists from two thousand entrants, and ended up in second place.

"He became quite a star," says Gillian. "It just shows you don't have to be a pedigree dog to be special!"

Gillian describes a typical day with Harvey, "Every morning, Harvey wakes me with a couple of 'kisses' then we do a little bit of yoga. After I shower and we have breakfast, Harvey and I go for a walk in the park. He loves chasing squirrels and rabbits but they are too fast for him. Harvey hasn't worked out how to climb a tree yet, but he's still trying! His favorite pastime is football (soccer). He doesn't wear his jacket in the park because that is 'his time,' but even then, Harvey is never far away from me. In fact, he is looking after me every minute of the day. At home, he is always with me, even in bed under the duvet!"

"I think I must be one of the luckiest people with uncontrolled epilepsy, to have a dog like Harvey and know that he is always there for me. He has given me back my confidence and given new meaning to my life. I can't imagine what life would be like without Harvey by my side."

SOLDIER

Virginia Muller found Soldier as an eight-week-old puppy. He was sitting in the dirt on the edge of the busy two-lane road that runs in front of her property in Porterville, California. The tiny pup was starved, dehydrated, infested with fleas and ticks, and had both eye and respiratory infections. He had very little hair on his body and was so filthy Virginia and her daughter couldn't even determine his color.

As they approached him, he looked into their faces and wobbled around on weak and spindly legs. The expression on his face was heartbreaking. He was depressed and defeated, but still hanging on to a glimmer of hope that these two-legged creatures would help him.

Virginia wrapped him in a towel, and she and her daughter set out for the veterinarian's clinic. Although neither of them spoke much during the ride, Virginia knew both were considering what to do with this little orphan. Between the two of them, they already cared for six rescued dogs and four rescued cats at what Virginia refers to as their "unsubsidized sanctuary." Throwaway pets are common in their area, which is the poorest county in California. Virginia contemplated her options. The pup could be peacefully and gently released from his short life, or Virginia could cut some more financial corners and give this homeless creature a chance.

At the small animal clinic, Virginia and the vet stared down at the examining table while the doctor waited for Virginia to tell him her decision. Suddenly, he broke the silence: "You know, if you can get him turned around, and if his ears stand upright, in about six months I think you'll have a really handsome German Shepherd."

The vet knew that Virginia wouldn't be impressed with the prospect of owning a purebred dog—she loved all animals, mutt or blueblood. He also knew that he was nudging her toward the decision she wanted to make all along. Virginia gathered the pup in her arms and took him home.

Soldier slowly responded to medical attention, love, and care and became not only handsome, but a calm, affectionate, obedient companion. Virginia had saved this dog's life; one day, Soldier would return the favor.

Virginia is diabetic and checks her blood sugar levels several times daily. One evening, she tested with a slightly lower glucose level than is desirable, but she wasn't concerned and decided not to have a snack before going to bed.

Around 4:00 A.M., she awoke to Soldier bumping and nudging her body repeatedly. As if from somewhere far away, she realized something was terribly wrong, and then vaguely understood she was slipping into a comalike sleep. She managed to pull herself up by holding onto Soldier's collar. Concentrating on each step and hanging onto the walls, she crept into the kitchen and stuffed some bread into her mouth, then ate some applesauce that she shakily dipped out of the jar with her fingers. She was drenched with sweat, trembling, disoriented, and had blurred vision. She sank into a chair by the phone, too weak to even make a call, as Soldier leaned against her knees. Putting her arms around his neck, she leaned forward and told him she would never leave him alone. The words seemed to give her strength as much as reassured her worried pet, and gradually she could feel her body responding as her blood sugar level rose.

She sat for what seemed like hours, gathering her strength as much from the presence of her faithful dog lying at her feet as from the food that was nourishing her body. Finally, when she was able to stand, she gathered her supplies and tested her glucose level. It was 41, dangerously lower than the optimum of 120. Virginia once again threw her arms around Soldier's neck, remembering the pitiful puppy she had once saved from certain death in the streets. No one could have predicted that when she saved his life, she also saved her own.

LADY

Rottweiler K-9 Officer Lady and her partner, Jim Crovetti, were known by schoolchildren throughout Iowa and Missouri by Lady's memorable motto, "Keep Your Paws Off Drugs!" Lady was a passive response K-9 who was trained to sniff out illegal substances and locate weapons and U.S. currency. She also traveled to schools, spreading the anti-drug message.

At home, Lady filled a different role. Jim had gotten Lady as a pup in 1991 at his doctor's suggestion following a heart attack. The doctor thought a dog would be a good incentive for Jim to take long walks and help with his initial recovery and weight loss. From a young age, Lady showed a special sensitivity to Jim's health. Whenever he experienced angina or similar distress, or his blood pressure was severely off, Lady wouldn't leave his side until his wife, Nancy, gave him medication or took some other action to help him. Ordinarily, Lady was content to stay in a central location in the house where she could watch Jim's activities, but if he didn't feel well, she rushed to his aid. She would follow him from room to room, even waiting outside the bathroom door until Nancy and Jim realized something was wrong.

Early in 2000, Lady became ill. She began to limp, and initial x-rays diagnosed osteosarcoma, a form of cancer. She underwent a successful amputation of her left front leg in May and began chemotherapy on June 5. On June 8, she was rushed back to the hospital as veterinarians and technicians tried rescue remedies, transfusions, and IVs in an effort to ease the devastating effects of the chemotherapy.

Despite her illness, Lady's love for her work never diminished. During one pre-op visit to the veterinary hospital, although she was besieged by pain, Lady greeted a class of elementary school children visiting the facility. She allowed each child to pet her and take one of her complimentary, collectible "Cop Cards." She also never gave up her job of monitoring the health of her best friend, Jim.

Sadly, the cancer proved too much for Lady. When she died on Father's Day, local and urban newspapers carried tributes acknowledging her accomplishments. She was recognized for her service to numerous law enforcement agencies in southern Iowa and northern Missouri as well as visits to hundreds of schools and civic groups nationwide. The *American Police Beat* newspaper also noted her numerous career and personal accomplishments in a September 2000 issue.

Lady's final recognition came posthumously when her primary vet, Dennis Woodruff, D.V.M., nominated her into the Iowa Veterinary Medical Association's Animal Hall of Fame (Professional Category). Dennis had more than a professional relationship with Lady—at one point during her illness he took her home for the weekend to ensure her twenty-four-hour care.

While Lady was missed by many, Jim grieved especially hard.

"They had been a team since her puppyhood, and for nearly nine years they were always together, forging a bond that was powerful to behold," says Nancy.

The October after Lady's death, Jim and Nancy visited some schools with next-in-line Heartland Canines, eager to carry on the legacy. But moving on was not easy. The "pawprint-shaped hole on their hearts" weighed most heavily on Jim. Jim often spoke of Lady's last hours, when he'd sat with her and prayed for her to survive.

"Jim told God if he could give her one more year, then the Lord could have them both," says Nancy.

"I truly believe the bond between them was so strong that after Lady died, Jim's heart literally broke. We have five other Rotts who are all special, but none were Lady."

That November, Jim died of a heart attack. The service on November 18 was for both of them; their ashes were laid side by side among the flowers, wreaths, and tributes. The inscription read "Lady, 8/22/91–6/18/00, and Jim, 12/2/30–11/14/00: Guardians on earth, and now my Guardian Angels." The following June, Jim and Lady were interred together at the K-9 Honor Wall.

"Two officers at the scene of Jim's death told me later that they were amazed to see a look of serenity on his face, almost a smile," says Nancy. "The only thing I can hope to believe is that he saw the Rainbow Bridge, and Lady was there waiting for him."

ZEUS

Some dogs show an uncanny ability to sense illness in their human partners. Zeus, the English Mastiff, is just such a dog.

Nell Wright first saw Zeus' picture on an English Mastiff rescue Web page and fell in love. When she read that he was eight years old, Nell was crushed. Mastiffs usually only live to about ten years old, and Nell didn't want to set herself up for a broken heart. She tried to forget him and checked out breeders in the hope of getting a puppy, but she couldn't forget Zeus' endearing face. Finally, Nell gave in to her heart and sent a family profile to Zeus' foster "mom" in the hopes of being approved for adoption.

Lila Wills e-mailed Nell back and told her Zeus was supposed to be adopted that weekend by a couple who had a ten-month-old Tibetan Mastiff, but she was sure they would be able to find Nell another Mastiff. Nell didn't tell Lila at the time, but she didn't want another Mastiff—she only wanted Zeus. Miraculously, the other adoption fell through, and Nell was approved to bring Zeus into her family.

Nell was thrilled to be able to provide a loving home for this sweet dog, whose numerous scars told of a life of abuse. Yet, despite his fear of punishment—he would drop to the floor if he thought Nell was even slightly upset with him—Zeus immediately settled into his new home.

Nell was told Zeus had probably been forced to participate in dog fights, which is where he received his scars. Yet, he has managed to forget the past, proving his gentle nature by carefully playing with puppies a fraction of his size. He also proved wonderful with children from the first day Nell brought him home, even though he initially was wary and aloof with adults. It often took Nell an hour to walk Zeus around the block because he wanted to stop and visit with all the children in the neighborhood.

Zeus soon showed an amazing sensitivity to Nell's moods, helping her through some especially difficult times in her life.

"He seems to know when I'm unhappy, and will come over, nudge me, wag his tail, and give me his paw until I stop feeling sorry for myself," said Nell. "Other times he'll do something to make me laugh. He'll bring me a toy or do this silly thing where he sticks his hind foot in his mouth and grins at me around it. He only does this when I'm down; it's like he's deliberately trying to make me laugh."

Although Nell appreciated Zeus' ability to cheer her up, she never imagined his sensitivity would one day save her life.

Nell was a brittle diabetic: She had difficulty controlling her blood sugar and had frequent insulin reactions that often occurred at night. In the past, she always woke up on her own during a reaction. One night a few months after she adopted Zeus, Nell was sound asleep when she was awakened at 3:00 A.M. to Zeus' loud barks and insistent shoves. In her disoriented state, she grumpily told Zeus to shut up and go lie down. But he refused and kept barking and pushing at his mistress with his nose. Nell tried to roll over and go back to sleep, but Zeus wouldn't allow it. Finally, Nell realized she was having a severe reaction. She grabbed the bag of gumdrops she kept by the bed and started popping the candies in her mouth. As soon as Zeus saw that Nell was following the procedure he had witnessed before in these situations, he stopped barking and lay back down next to the bed.

Nell said although Zeus had acted concerned on other occasions, she had always been aware that an insulin reaction was coming and had taken the proper precautions. If this perceptive dog hadn't alerted his owner to her reaction and kept pestering her until she took action, Nell's diabetic reaction would most likely have turned fatal.

Prologue: Shortly before this book went to print, I received word from Nell's mother that Zeus had died of old age while being treated at the local veterinary school's hospital. When Nell received word at her office of Zeus' death, she left work, went home, and wrote her mother a note saying she couldn't bear to live without her companion. Nell's mother later found Nell curled up in Zeus' dog bed—Nell had died on the same day as her beloved dog.

"Zeus was the only thing that kept her going," says Nell's mother. "I believe she truly died of a broken heart."

CHAPTER 6

DOGS AND KIDS

Many dogs seem to show extra compassion toward children. Perhaps they sense the vulnerability and innocence of children and feel a sense of duty to protect them. Whatever the reason, there is no greater bond than the friendship between a child and a dog.

TOBY

It's always a little unnerving when a couple decides to add a two-legged child to a household that has only known the four-legged variety. Will the resident dog accept the new baby? Will there be resentment?

Jeanette Stafford of Freehold, New Jersey, and her husband contemplated these worries when Jeanette discovered she was pregnant. For three years, their Yorkshire Terrier, Toby, had been their "baby." Jeannette and her husband had showered all their love and attention onto Toby. But now the dog would have to share their affections with a new addition. Friends warned them that Toby would be jealous, and some even advised that they get rid of her before the baby arrived. Despite these well-meaning comments from friends and family, Jeanette and her husband believed that there was nothing to fear.

From the moment baby Keith arrived, Toby was enthralled. She would faithfully watch the bassinet from her vantage point on top of the Stafford's bed and would run to get them if Keith cried.

With each passing month, Keith and Toby became closer and closer. Jeanette remembers the day when the three of them were enjoying a play session in the middle of the bed. Keith got up on his knees, reached out, and took his first tentative crawl—he was trying to reach Toby.

Jeanette was thrilled that Keith and Toby had become best buddies. Still, she had yet to learn the extent of Toby's devotion to her human "sibling."

One day, Jeanette was getting ready to take Keith and Toby for a walk. With Keith safely in her arms, she opened the gate blocking the stairs of their second-floor apartment. She was interrupted by the jangle of the phone. She stepped into the kitchen and put Keith down on the floor next to her. After what seemed like only a moment, she suddenly heard Toby making a noise that could only be described as a scream. Jeanette glanced down—Keith was gone.

Jeanette raced in the direction of Toby's screams to see Keith teetering at the top of the stairway. But there was

Toby, blocking his fall with her diminutive body. As Keith's balance shifted, and he tipped toward the flight of twenty-six steps, Toby pushed against him with all her might, screaming a cry that Jeanette had never heard before. Jeanette quickly scooped up Keith and pulled Toby close, shaking from the realization that her heroic little dog may have saved her baby's life.

Toby lived the next fifteen years of his life as Keith's friend and protector. Although Keith was an only child, he later said that he was never lonely because he had Toby.

On the rare occasions that the family went out without her, Toby sat at the top of the stairs, waiting for them to return. She seemed to view the steps with a new, healthy respect after her chilling experience, perhaps remembering their potential danger and the day she had rescued her true best friend.

CONNOR

When Carole Krajeski of Streamwood, Illinois, received a call asking if she would foster a puppy for a local rescue organization, her first thought was to pass. She had recently rescued a three-month-old pot-bellied pig, who was taking up all her time and skills. Before she could answer, "No," the person on the other end of the line was pleading. "We have so few dog foster homes and nobody can take a puppy right now. And he's a huge puppy. Can't you take him just for a little while?"

"Oh, sure," Carole agreed. "Bring him over. What's one more, right?"

That was nearly nine years ago, and Connor is still with her.

He certainly was a huge puppy. With his white coloring, gold patches, and big dark eyes, Carole's best guess was that he was a Great Pyrenees/Golden Retriever mix. His personality combined the sweetness and trainability of a Golden with the single-minded devotion of a Pyrenees.

The police had found Connor abandoned on the street. He was a sweet, easygoing puppy, a breeze to house-train, and willing to do whatever Carole asked. Within a week, it was obvious that Connor was there to stay.

One of Carole's sons took Connor to a puppy kindergarten class that Carole taught. That eight-week class was the only formal training Connor received, yet he unfailingly obeys all commands. From the beginning, it was as if he were simply refreshing his memory about things he already knew. By the age of five months, he was visiting the local senior center and accompanying Carole when she brought all types of pets to local kindergartens, Boy Scout meetings, and the Head Start program.

Connor loved everyone he met, especially children. He would sprawl on the floor, with his tail swishing happily, as kids climbed all over him. Connor grew steadily, finally topping out at 130 pounds.

When Carole's first granddaughter was born, Connor immediately fell in love. When she began to walk, he dutifully followed her every step. He often drooled in her hair, causing her to elbow him in the chest and order him to "Get back!" Of course, he would obediently do as she commanded. Carole once discovered her granddaughter studiously brushing Connor's teeth, one little fist clutching his lip while the other vigorously cleaned those large pearly whites. He sat there patiently until she was done.

Connor was always a gentle giant, with one memorable exception. One day, Carole's twelve-year-old daughter and seven-year-old son decided to take Connor and Chiara, the family's pit bull, for a walk. Two blocks from home, they encountered a man and a woman walking toward them. When the couple was yards away, Connor stopped and refused to budge. His gaze was fixed on the man. Carole's daughter tried to urge him forward, but he refused to take another step. As the couple got closer, Connor moved to stand in front of the young girl, blocking her path. Again, he refused to budge. Sweet, trusting Chiara was wagging her tail, wanting to greet the two people who were approaching.

When the couple called out a greeting, Connor responded with a menacing growl. Now the children were worried. Connor had never growled at anyone in his life. They turned and hurried home.

Connor has never shown the slightest aggression toward anyone since that occasion. He's a senior citizen now, but still greets unfamiliar children by lying down so they can pet him. He's happy to see everyone; friends and strangers alike.

Carole says, "I've never had a moment that I regretted taking him home. As a matter of fact, I think God sent this guardian angel to us for a reason. You see, the man he growled at that day was a convicted child molester."

THE TINIEST PUPPY

Roger Kiser Sr. of Brunswick, Georgia, shared a story of the immediate connection between a boy and a puppy, who discovered they had more than youth in common.

The night of the puppy's birth was a long and stressful one for both Roger and the puppy's mother, Precious. Roger's black Cocker Spaniel was having a difficult labor. Roger lay on the floor with her all night, watching her every movement in case he needed to rush her to the veterinarian.

After six hours, the puppies started to arrive. The first-born was a black and white particolored dog. The second and third puppies were tan and brown. The fourth and fifth, like the first, were spotted black and white.

"One, two, three, four, five," Roger counted to himself. He walked down the hallway to wake up his wife, Judy, to tell her the puppies had finally arrived and everything was fine.

As Roger and Judy walked back down the hallway and into the spare bedroom, Roger noticed that a sixth puppy had been born and was now lying all by itself by the side of the cage. Roger picked up the tiny puppy and gently placed it on top of the large pile of nursing puppies. Instantly, Precious pushed this new puppy away from the rest of the group and refused to recognize it as a member of her family.

"Something's wrong," said Judy.

Roger picked up the puppy and looked into its tiny face. His heart sank when he saw that the little puppy was harelipped and couldn't close its mouth. Roger knew the poor odds this puppy faced, but he also knew he had to do his best to save the helpless animal. The next day, Roger took the puppy to the vet and was told there was nothing he could do unless he was willing to spend $1,000 to try to surgically correct the defect. The vet said the puppy would die because he couldn't suckle.

After returning home, Roger and Judy determined they couldn't afford to spend that kind of money without getting some type of assurance from the vet that the puppy really did have a chance to live. Despite the uncertainty over the puppy's future, Roger purchased a syringe and fed the pup by hand every two hours for more than ten days.

When the puppies were five weeks old, Roger placed an ad in the newspaper, and within a week, he had taken deposits on all the puppies except the one with the deformity. Despite the veterinarian's warnings, the puppy had learned to eat soft canned food on his own, and he was thriving.

Late that afternoon, one of Roger's neighbors, a retired schoolteacher, approached him. She had read in the paper that Roger and Judy had puppies for sale and wanted to buy one for her grandson. Roger told her that all the puppies had been sold, but that he would let her know if he heard of anyone else who had a Cocker Spaniel for sale.

Within days, all but one of the puppies had been picked up by their new owners. This left Roger and Judy with one brown and tan Cocker as well as the harelipped puppy. Two more days passed without Roger hearing anything from the gentleman who had placed a deposit on the brown and tan puppy. Roger telephoned his neighbor and told her he had one puppy left, and she was welcome to come and look at him. The woman thanked him and said she would pick up her grandson and come over around 8:00 that evening.

Judy and Roger were eating supper when they heard a knock on the front door. It was the man who had originally put a deposit on the brown and tan puppy. Roger filled out the paperwork for the dog, the man paid his balance due, and happily left with his new puppy. Judy and Roger exchanged glances. Neither knew what to do or say if their neighbor showed up with her grandson.

At exactly 8:00, the schoolteacher arrived. Her grandson stood shyly behind her. Roger explained that a man who already had a claim on the puppy had showed up just an hour before, and there were no puppies left.

"I'm sorry, Jeffery," the neighbor told her grandson. "They sold all the puppies."

Suddenly, the harelipped puppy Roger and Judy had left in the bedroom began to yelp.

"My puppy! My puppy!" yelled the little boy, as he ran out from behind his grandmother. Roger caught his breath as he saw the boy clearly for the first time. Like the puppy, the boy, too, was harelipped. Jeffery ran past Roger and down the hallway to reach the puppy, who still was yelping. When the three adults reached the bedroom, the boy was holding the puppy in his arms. The puppy, oblivious to the little boy's deformity, was enthusiastically licking his face.

The boy looked up at his grandmother and said, "Look Grandma. They sold all the puppies except the pretty one, and he looks just like me."

Roger and Judy felt tears filling their eyes as they looked at each other, unsure of what to do.

"Is this puppy for sale?" asked the teacher, fighting back tears of her own.

"My grandma told me these kind of puppies are real expensive and that I have to take real good care of it," said the little boy.

Roger felt his doubts melt away. "Yes ma'am. This puppy is for sale," he told the teacher.

The woman opened her purse, and Roger could see several $100 bills sticking out of her wallet. He reached over and pushed her hand back down into her purse so she wouldn't pull out the money.

"How much do you think this puppy is worth?" he asked the boy.

"About a dollar?" the boy answered hesitantly.

"No. This puppy is very, very expensive," Roger replied.

"More than a dollar?" he asked.

"I'm afraid so," Roger told him.

The boy stood there, pressing the small puppy against his cheek.

"We could not possibly take less than two dollars for this puppy. Like you said, it's the pretty one," said Judy, squeezing Roger's hand.

The teacher took out two worn dollars and handed them to the young boy.

"It's your dog now, Jeffery. You pay the man," she told him.

To this day, Roger marvels at the young boy and the puppy who found the beauty in each other that many others refused to see.

TOBY

Judi Perrin is a language arts teacher in Marietta, Ohio. During a Humane Society Awareness assembly at her school, she adopted a German Shorthaired Retriever/ Dalmatian mix puppy. Toby has proven an irreplaceable companion not only to Judi, but also to the students she teaches.

The day Judi walked into the assembly, she had no idea she would walk out with a puppy. "I didn't think I would get another dog, but there he was, about eight weeks old and as cute as all puppies are known to be," says Judi. "His ears were solid olive brown and soft as well-worn gloves. The rest of him was a wagging tail attached to many spots and speckles."

As Toby got older, his friendly nature made him a perfect candidate to become a therapy dog. Shortly after completing his training for this endeavor, Judi began to experience vision problems. She was walking home with Toby one day when her vision disappeared completely. Toby immediately took over, stepping slightly ahead of Judi and leaning against her to provide support and balance as they cautiously made their way home.

When Judi was diagnosed with visual migraines, she looked to Toby to help her deal with her condition. She began training Toby as her service dog to aid her mobility. Toby seemed to know what his job was, and he did it happily. For her part, Judi found that Toby gave her the confidence she needed to continue living life as she always had.

Toby helped Judi navigate all the obstacles fully sighted people take for granted. "Stairs did not seem quite as scary if I had four extra feet beside me," says Judi.

When school began again in the fall, Toby accompanied Judi to the classroom. The eighth-grade students whom Judi worked with loved having the dog in their room. They fed him treats, played with him, petted him, and told him their secrets. "In exchange, the students had a 75-pound package of unconditional love in the classroom," says Judi.

As the school year progressed, one student asked if he could spend most of study hall with Toby. The student, who had failed several grades, seemed like a different child when he was with Toby. He would sit quietly next to the dog and pat him, talk to him, check his feet for any minor cuts, and feed Toby his special treats. Once outside the study hall, however, the boy would once again become rebellious and disruptive.

One day, the student's special education teacher approached Judi and asked if he could remain in Judi's study hall for the rest of the year. Judi agreed, and she and the special education teacher set down some ground rules for the boy. He could stay in the study hall with Toby if he behaved himself both in and out of Judi's classroom and if his teachers reported that he had completed all his work for that day. In addition, Judi told him, he had to follow her corrections for proper speech and only give Toby commands the way that Judi had taught them. When the boy asked why, Judi responded, "I don't want Toby to pick up any bad habits!" The boy grinned and agreed to the conditions to continue seeing Toby.

Shortly afterward, the boy and his grandparents attended a parent–teacher conference to discuss his progress. The boy's special education teacher invited Toby to attend as well. The formerly rough young man sat in his chair with tears in his eyes as the teacher recounted his amazing academic and behavioral accomplishments since Toby had come into his life. At the end of the conference, the student asked Toby to come closer so that he could pat him. Toby walked over to the boy, then placed his paws on the boy's shoulders and showered him with kisses.

"There wasn't a dry eye in the room," says Judi. "After fifteen years of teaching at the school, I never attended a more satisfying conference than the one 'held' by Toby."

SHETLAND SHEEPDOGS AND KIDS

Susan Traut of Elyria, Ohio, is the mother of Orrin, her nine-year-old son who has high-functioning autism. She also owns several Shetland Sheepdogs who help Orrin cope with his disability.

"Owning Shelties has had a major impact on Orrie's life and on the rest of the family," says Susan. "Do these Shelties know that he is different? I certainly believe so."

One of Susan's dogs, Chance, is particularly sensitive to Orrie's needs.

"When Orrie is in one of his hyper states, Chance will go to him to be petted, which calms Orrie down and enables him to focus."

Susan also credits her dogs with helping Orrie with the schoolwork that is so difficult for him.

"Although Orrie is in third grade, he was unable to read until this year. He now sits on the floor and reads to Chance and the other Shelties. They seem to love to be read to, and because they seem so interested, Orrie is very enthusiastic and has come a long way."

Joyce Hanson of Gervais, Oregon, describes the story of one of her Shetland Sheepdogs who was adopted by a woman looking for a dog to replace her son's dog, who had just died of old age. The boy had several health problems and was scheduled to go in for surgery. The doctors felt that getting a new dog would boost the boy emotionally. Joyce gave them the dog on a trial basis to see how things would work out.

The next day, Joyce received a call from the mother, who was crying. Joyce feared the worst until she heard the reason for the woman's tears.

"She explained that the dog was there to stay," says Joyce. "The night before, a few hours after they got home, the boy went into a seizure in his bedroom. The Sheltie ran to the parents and refused to leave them until they followed him. The dog then ran back to the boy and lay beside him until the parents stabilized him. He saved the boy's life."

The Sheltie now accompanies the boy to school every day and alerts the teachers before the boy has a seizure, enabling them to give him the medicine he carries in his backpack. This wonderful little dog was also given permission to be in the boy's room at the hospital when he goes in for surgery. The doctors say the boy's chances for recovery are great because of the change in his attitude since this dog came into his life.

What makes this story even more amazing is that the Sheltie almost didn't live past puppyhood. He, like the pup in Roger Kiser's story, was born with a cleft palate. While many breeders would have put the puppy down, Joyce tube-fed him until he was four months old. At that time, her vet performed the expensive corrective surgery at cost. At six months of age, the Sheltie became lame, and it was discovered that the blood vessels around his hip ball had not formed correctly, causing the hip ball to disintegrate in the socket. Once again, Joyce opted for surgery, and the ball was removed to prevent any more pain. Joyce muses, "One life that many considered not worth sparing was saved, and in return, that life saved another!"

BORDER COLLIES AND KIDS

Kathy Morgan, of New South Wales, Australia, says her Border Collies are true guardians to her children.

"One of my sons started walking early; at eight months old. One of my Border Collies, Ziggy, let my son hold onto her neck and together they would walk. She would take tiny steps so he could keep up. She would also walk between him and the furniture so if he fell, he would fall on her. Now my son is four years old, and Ziggy is his constant companion; he tells everyone that Ziggy is his best friend."

Ziggy also is the guardian of her ten-year-old son. "One day when my older son was four years old, I was doing housework and Ziggy came in and stared at me and barked. She did this for a few times until I realized that she actually wanted to show me something. I followed her out back and found my child lighting matches and paper in a barrel. Honestly, the look on her face when she knew she had done the right thing was priceless, and the look on my son's face when he realized he had been busted by the dog was even better. He no longer plays with matches, but she still follows him everywhere just to keep an eye on him."

Nanette Bragg of Alice Springs, Northern Territory, Australia, also experienced firsthand the Border Collie's protective instinct.

"I was on the phone and had not noticed my youngest child, Michaela, leave the shed. I heard my dogs give a very strange bark, and I thought they had cornered a snake. I always got rid of the snakes, so I went to check. My youngest female Border Collie was bounding on the verandah and ran off toward the back of the property as soon as I showed my face, so I followed her. As I got closer, I realized my other dogs were there, too. My oldest male was standing in front of Michaela, barking ferociously at her, and my oldest female had a very firm grip on her diaper. Not more than a meter behind them was a long unfenced drop into the valley below our property. My heart was in my mouth as I realized what almost happened. I picked Michaela up and the dogs settled down and wandered back to the house. If not for those unbelievably loyal and protective Border Collies, I dread to think of the consequences of my poor care."

BONES

Shanna Neal of Kenna, West Virginia, has firsthand experience of the Boxer breed's legendary love for children.

"My Boxer, Bones, was about two years old when my grandson, Kevin, made his entrance into the world. Kevin immediately took to Bones and vice versa. Bones was very protective of this child and even growled once at my daughter because she played too roughly with Kevin and he squealed."

Like Ziggy the Border Collie, Bones taught Kevin how to walk. "Kevin would hold onto Bones' docked tail and Bones would pull him to his feet. I had never seen a dog that would allow a child to hang onto his tail, let alone seek to have it abused. Bones would slowly walk across the floor and Kevin would follow, hanging onto this little stub. If Kevin lost his balance and sat down, the dog would go and lick his face and then sit down with his back to Kevin and wait for him to grab that stub again before standing up and walking some more. I don't know how many times poor Bones had to allow me to wash 'stickies' off his tail, but I do know that when Kevin was able to walk on his own, he and Bones were inseparable."

THOR

Anita Duhon of Lake Charles, Louisiana, tells a wonderful story of how her Border Collie, Thor, touched the heart of a troubled little girl. Anita and Thor were on their way out to the parking garage of the hospital after a therapy visit when a young couple with two children walked toward them. The boy, who was about eight years old, stepped alongside his sister to shield her from Thor. The girl stopped and hesitated to pass the dog in the walkway. Thor and the girl stared at each other, then Thor decided to act. He seemed to sense the fear in the little girl and wanted to reassure her. He stared at the children, picked up a paw and waved.

"The surprise on those faces was precious," says Anita. Anita then showed them the hand signals for "sit," "down," and "wave," and asked them if they would like to try the commands. Thor did whatever the children asked of him, then sat directly in front of the little girl and silently looked at her with his soft brown eyes. The girl petted him from ear to ear, head to tail, and he sat perfectly still.

"So where was the miracle in all of this?" says Anita. "Their mom told me that the little girl had been attacked by a dog more than a year ago, and she had a metal plate in her head as a result. The brother had gotten very protective of his little sister, and both were very afraid of dogs. This was the first time they had petted a dog since the attack. I saw the Border Collie magic displayed right in front of me: the magic of a therapy dog."

CHAPTER 7

ALL GOD'S CREATURES

We all love stories of dogs showing compassion in their relationships with their human companions. But dogs don't reserve their compassion strictly for the humans in their lives; many dogs have also performed compassionate acts toward other animals. From two Poodles who helped each other cope with their disabilities to a Shetland Sheepdog who led his owner to his lost and dying companion, the dogs described in this chapter show a humanlike love for their fellow canine.

A dog's compassion for other animals goes beyond its brothers, and many dogs have shown love for other species. This includes dogs who have adopted kittens or other orphaned animal babies, and those who ignore their natural instinct to hunt and instead choose to befriend such prey as rabbits and birds.

HELPMATE POODLES

Anne Page of Houston, Texas, was once asked, "Can you train one dog to be a guide dog for another?" She answered by relating this amazing story of canine companionship and compassion, which first appeared in her newspaper, *Canine Classified.*

One night many years ago, Anne was visiting her friend Judy, who had two male Toy Poodles that were raised together from puppyhood. In their twilight years, one had become blind and the other had gone deaf. Anne witnessed their unique arrangement to help each other deal with their disabilities.

The two dogs were napping on a cushion on the floor when Judy's mother went into the kitchen, picked up the dog dishes, and started to fill them with kibble. The blind dog immediately woke up and nudged the deaf dog until he awoke as well. The deaf dog looked across the family room to the kitchen and saw what Judy's mother was doing, then he nudged the blind dog. Both stood up, and the deaf dog took the end of the blind dog's collar strap in his mouth. They headed to the kitchen together to gobble down their dinners side by side.

When they had completed their meals, the deaf dog led the blind dog to the back door, and they went out through the dog door into the yard. A few minutes later, Judy and Anne went outside to call the dogs in for the night. The diminutive Poodles were standing a few feet apart investigating the bushes. The blind dog raised his head when he heard Judy's voice, sniffed the air, then turned around and walked toward the deaf dog until he reached his furry friend. The deaf dog then took the blind dog by the collar and led him to the dog door. Anne relates, "It was one of the most touching scenes I have ever witnessed between dogs."

This incredible partnership lasted until one day the deaf dog was rushed into emergency surgery to remove a rotted tooth that had caused a gum infection. Old age and the advanced infection proved too much for the valiant Poodle, and he died on the operating table. Judy and her family were heartbroken over the death of their beloved dog, and worried that their other Poodle would be lost without his constant companion. They did their best to console the other dog, and even tried to take on the role their deaf Poodle had performed, all to no avail. The blind dog grieved so deeply that they were not surprised when he died in his sleep a few nights later.

Anne stresses that nobody trained these dogs to assist one another. They began to compensate for each other's losses at about age twelve, and each continued to help his canine soulmate until their deaths a week apart, just shy of their seventeenth birthdays.

EMMA

Emma the Doberman is another dog with sight problems. She has been blind since birth, but she too has her own guide dog. Amy, another Doberman who lives with Emma in Ottawa, Canada, wears a bell attached to her collar, and Emma follows the sound. It is likely that without Amy, Emma would be restricted from doing many of the activities she enjoys now. With Amy, Emma not only negotiates walls, furniture, and people but also navigates rocky slopes, swims, and goes shopping with her owners.

SKIPPER

Several years ago, Lela Roby of Leavenworth, Indiana, had three canine companions: a Rhodesian Ridgeback, a Shetland Sheepdog (Skipper), and a Belgian Sheepdog (Chauncey). Every day, the three dogs happily roamed Lela's forty-acre farm. Although the Belgian had lost a front leg to bone cancer, he was quite nimble and typically had no problem keeping up with his buddies.

One day, however, the dogs took off after a deer and only the Ridgeback and Sheltie returned. The family searched for hours and alerted the neighbors—all farmers living a half-mile to three-quarters of a mile apart—to Chauncey's disappearance. Soon darkness fell, and the search was suspended for the evening. That night, there was a thunderstorm. Lela's heart ached, wondering where her beloved companion was during the downpour. Was he hurt? Had he found shelter? She feared the worst, but she was not about to give up hope.

The search continued the next day. As Lela searched, Skipper trotted faithfully along next to her, watching her every move. At one point, Lela said to Skipper, "Where's Chauncey? Find Chauncey!" She admits the pleas were more out of desperation than any belief the Sheltie could actually help. Skipper leaped up and down. He seemed to understand that Lela needed something from him, but he wasn't quite sure what that something was. He continued trotting excitedly beside her, his tail waving back and forth with each bounce, watching his mistress intently.

Lela and Skipper traveled across a field and came upon a barbed wire fence. Lela glanced down and was shocked to find a piece of Chauncey's long black fur caught in the fence. She unsnarled it, held it under Skipper's nose, and once again commanded, "Find Chauncey!" Without hesitation, Skipper bolted across the meadow. Lela ran after him, her heart pounding. Maybe her little Sheltie really could help!

They came to the woods bordering the field, and Lela slipped down the steep embankment, trying to keep up with her nimble scout. At the bottom of the hill was a shallow stream. Skipper turned right and started along the stream, then hesitated, looking perplexed. Lela caught up to the Sheltie and once again held the fur under his nose. This was all the reminder he needed. Skipper splashed across the stream, then followed its course as it wound through the trees. Suddenly, Skipper stopped and turned to look back at Lela.

Lela could hear Chauncey whimpering before she saw him, about 15 feet ahead. It appeared that Chauncey had slipped on a rock while crossing the stream and had broken his hind leg. With only two good legs remaining, he was unable to move at all. As Lela rushed to her injured pet's side, Skipper looked up at her expectantly as if to say, "Is this what you wanted? Here he is. I found him for you!" Lela petted his soft head and told him how good he was, which was all the reward he needed.

Chauncey weakly lifted his head at his owner's voice, then laid it back down. Although the 75-pound Belgian weighed three-quarters of his owner's weight, she didn't hesitate to lift him, as gently as she could, and begin the arduous trek home. She struggled up the steep incline, stopping to rest once or twice with the dog lying across her legs. Finally, she made it to the top and across the fields to the house.

Lela and her husband, Rob, rushed Chauncey to the veterinarian, who performed surgery on Chauncey's shattered leg. But the trauma proved too much for this brave dog, who had survived what seemed like insurmountable odds in the past. Sadly, Chauncey succumbed to a massive infection several days later.

The Robys were devastated at the loss of one of their best friends. Chauncey had been through so much. After he beat the cancer, he had seemed almost invincible. Yet, in their grief, the Robys found comfort in being reunited with Chauncey and making his last hours more bearable, returning all the love and affection he had shown them during his too-short life.

"To this day, I shudder to think of the horrible, slow death my faithful companion would have suffered were it not for the intelligence of my wonderful Skipper," says Lela. "And every day I thank my loyal little Sheltie, who wanted to do nothing but please his mistress, and was so happy with himself for having fulfilled his mission."

JETHRO

Marc Bekoff is no stranger to the idea that dogs are capable of showing emotion. In fact, Marc—who is a professor of animal behavior at the University of Colorado,

Boulder—is among a group of scientists trying to prove in scientific terms that dogs and other animals have emotions. The story of Marc's dog, Jethro, first appeared in his book on animal emotions called *The Smile of a Dolphin*.

Marc rescued Jethro from the local humane society when the dog was about nine months old. Jethro appears to be a Rottweiler/German Shepherd mix, with perhaps a little hound thrown in. He is black and tan, somewhat barrel-chested, with dripping jowls and long floppy ears. From the start, Jethro was a low-key, gentle, well-mannered companion. He didn't chase other animals around Marc's mountain home, and he loved to just hang out and watch the world around him. He made the perfect field assistant as Marc studied various birds living around his house.

One day, while Marc was sitting inside the house, he heard Jethro come to the front door. Instead of whining as he usually did when he wanted to come in, the dog just sat motionless, his soulful eyes begging Marc to let him in. Marc looked at him and noticed a small object in his mouth. At first, Marc thought Jethro had killed a bird, which was very unlike the mild-mannered canine. When Marc opened the door, however, Jethro proceeded to drop a very young bunny at his feet. Although the tiny rabbit was drenched in Jethro's saliva, it was still moving. Marc didn't see any injuries, but the bunny obviously needed warmth, food, and love or it wouldn't survive. Jethro looked at Marc with wide-eyes, as if he wanted Marc to praise him for being such a Good Samaritan. Marc obliged, amazed that Jethro had transported the bunny so gently. Marc assumed the bunny's mother wasn't coming back; most likely she fell prey to one of the coyotes, red foxes, or mountain lions that Marc occasionally glimpsed around his house.

When Marc picked up the bunny, Jethro became concerned. The dog tried to snatch the rabbit from Marc's hands, whined, and followed Marc around as he gathered a box, a blanket, and some water and food. Marc carefully placed the bunny in the box, and wrapped her in the blanket. He decided to simply call her Bunny. After awhile, he put some mashed up carrots, celery, and lettuce near her, and she tried to eat. He also made sure that she knew where the water was. All the while, Jethro stood as a sentinel behind Marc, watching his every move. At first, Marc worried Jethro might go for the bunny or the food, but he was content to just observe the little fluff ball slowly moving around in her new home.

When Marc felt he had done all he could, he started to walk away, calling Jethro to join him, but the dog wouldn't budge. Jethro usually came to Marc immediately, especially when he offered the dog a treat, but this time Jethro refused to leave the bunny's box. He remained there for the rest of the day.

That evening, Marc dragged Jethro out for his nightly walk. When they returned, Jethro ran straight to the box and curled up beside it. Marc tried to get Jethro to go to his usual sleeping spot, but the dog refused. He seemed to be saying, "No way, I'm staying here." He slept the entire night in that spot, guarding his bunny. Jethro adopted Bunny as his personal charge during the two weeks that Marc nursed her back to health.

Finally, the day came when Marc introduced Bunny to the outdoors. He and Jethro walked to the east side of the house, where Marc released her from her box and watched her slowly make her way into a woodpile. She was cautious; her senses seemed to be overwhelmed by the new sights, sounds, and odors she was encountering. Bunny remained in the woodpile for about an hour until she boldly stepped out to begin life as a full-fledged rabbit. Jethro watched from a few feet away. He never took his eyes off Bunny and never tried to approach her. It was as if he was lending his assurance that he was there if she needed him.

Bunny hung around the yard for a few months. Every time Marc let Jethro out of the house, the dog immediately ran to the spot where she was released. When he reached the woodpile, he cocked his head and moved it from side to side, looking for Bunny.

Marc isn't sure what became of Bunny. Other bunnies and adults rabbits have come and gone, and Jethro looks at each of them, perhaps wondering if one of them is his Bunny. He tries to get as close as he can, but he never chases them or threatens them in any way.

Several years after Jethro saved Bunny, he ran up to Marc with another wet animal in his mouth. Marc asked him to drop it, expecting to find another bunny. This time, however, Jethro had rescued a young bird that had flown into a window. It was stunned and just needed to regain its senses. Marc held it in his hands for a few minutes, while his dog, in true Jethro fashion, watched the bird's every move. When Marc thought the bird was ready to fly, he placed it on the porch railing. Jethro approached the bird, cautiously sniffed it, then stepped back and watched it fly away.

These two selfless acts truly seem to demonstrate Jethro's compassion for fellow animals.

"Jethro has saved two animals from death," says Marc. "He could easily have gulped each down with little effort. But you don't do that to friends, do you?"

CATS AND DOGS

Many dogs haven't heard the conventional wisdom that dogs and cats don't mix. Many not only accept the felines in their lives, they also become best friends with cats.

Cyndee Walklet of Columbia, South Carolina, tells the story of an abandoned kitten she found in a parking lot. She decided to bring the three-week-old, half-pound kitten home so she could bottle-feed him around the clock. At the time, she owned five female Shetland Sheepdogs and one male. She was sure at least one of the females would show a mothering instinct and help her care for the kitten.

When she got home, all six dogs gathered around the cat carrier. The kitten just sniffed back at them—he had no fear. Once Cyndee let him out, the five females ran to the farthest corners of the house!

"I picked up the little guy and called to my male blue merle Sheltie, Merlin, who joined me on the bed. He lay right down, and the little kitty immediately headed for the mountain of blue fur in front of him. I could hear his little purr as he nuzzled at Merlin's stomach, looking for access to the milk that was definitely not there. Much to my surprise, Merlin rolled over on his back and let Yoda, as the kitten became known, climb up and over his chest, explore his face, and head back to Merlin's tummy. He latched onto a nipple. Merlin rolled his eyes at me as if to say, 'Mom, get it off of there!' I decided it was time to get the bottle ready, and I'm sure Merlin agreed!"

"Once his tummy was full, Yoda headed back to his gentle friend. Merlin was still lying patiently on his back, and Yoda climbed up onto his chest. Yoda snuggled under one of Merlin's folded front paws, curled up, and slipped into a sound sleep, purring contentedly—a speck of white afloat in a sea of blue Sheltie fur."

When Lynn Renor of Madison, Wisconsin, took in a stray kitten, she also witnessed the strong mothering instinct of a Rottweiler.

"Isadora was one of a litter of four and was by far the tiniest kitten," says Lynn. "She had hookworms, whipworms, every worm imaginable, plus an upper respiratory infection. She was going to be put to sleep."

Lynn brought the kitten home to try to nurse her back to health. She felt confident her Rottweiler, Sorcha, would get along with the kitten, but she never imagined to what extent.

"Whenever Isadora would meow, Sorcha would come running and start licking her. There was a lot of mutual bathing and cuddling going on!" Sorcha's penchant for kittens in distress didn't stop there. When a friend of Lynn's took in a litter of three-week-old strays, Sorcha loved to help out. "When the kittens would eat, they would get covered in formula. Sorcha would lie down, hold each kitten between her front paws, and lick it clean. Eventually, she would gather all the kittens and nestle them between her paws."

Sherri Meinholz of DeForest, Wisconsin, has seen a cat-loving nature in her Rottie, Rahja. According to Sherri, "When Rahja was one-and-a-half years old, I was taking care of two litters of newborn kittens. Rahja not only cleaned them off, she also licked their rears like a mother cat would to make them to go to the bathroom. She is so attached to cats that when I bring her in to the vet clinic where I work and strange cats hiss at her, she lies down and cries."

Shadow, a Labrador Retriever, who lives in Ireland, adopted five kittens whose mother was run over by a car. Shadow immediately noticed the three-month-old kittens crying for their mother and decided to take over the job. The Lab cleaned the kittens, slept with them, and supervised them while they played.

BENTLEY

Lynn Uram of Canonsburg, Pennsylvania, says her Shetland Sheepdog Bentley is particularly empathetic not only to people, but also to other animals as well.

"When we brought Parker, our other Sheltie, home after having him neutered, Bentley circled Parker's crate for an hour, howling and crying the entire time. He stopped only long enough to put his paw through the crate bars to touch Parker's back as if to say, 'It's okay, Buddy!' Bentley has a sweet and loving nature with all creatures. He's even been known to delicately pick up ladybugs and gently lay them on our laps!"

THE LOVE OF ROTTWEILERS

Marianne Harrison is the proud owner of six Rottweilers and an English Bulldog. Many female Rottweilers display an uncanny maternal instinct, whether with their own pups, another dog's pups, or even baby animals of another species. Marianne experienced this firsthand when her one female, Sadie, got upset because one of the other Rottie's puppies was crying.

"Sadie jumped right in the whelping box with them and scooped up half of the puppies between her paws as if to say, 'Here Elsa, I'll take half and help you out!'"

Nelson Abdullah of Fort Mitchell, Kentucky, has a Rottweiler who not only loves cats, but also appreciates wildlife of all types.

"In our house we have two cats and three Rottweilers and everyone lives in perfect harmony. One of the cats, a six-year-old female named Casey, goes outside and hunts every day. Since we live in a populated suburban community, we seldom see any wildlife other than birds, squirrels, chipmunks, moles, garden snakes, and an occasional rabbit. One day, my wife and I were in the backyard with one of the Rotties, Felony. Casey spotted a rabbit in the next-door neighbor's backyard and began to stalk it in her usual fashion. She crouched down and slowly inched her way across the grass toward the rabbit. As she made her way toward us and the rabbit, the bunny spotted her and realized it was surrounded.

"The rabbit had to choose which was the least dangerous of these four creatures—one of the humans, the cat, or the Rottweiler. In a few short hops, it headed straight for the Rottweiler, and for a moment, it sat in front of Felony with its little nose twitching away. Felony lowered her huge head and went nose to nose with this little creature before it hopped right past her and bounded off across our property."

CHAPTER 8

DO DOGS GRIEVE?

There is perhaps no greater evidence of compassion than grief. The dogs described in this chapter show an almost human capacity to mourn the passing of their loved ones.

ANDRE

Barbara Marshall's breed of choice is the Bearded Collie. When her mother, Barbara Allen, decided she needed a canine companion in her life, she too was attracted to this energetic, happy-go-lucky breed, but Barbara felt a Beardie was too large for her mother to handle. Barbara searched for a more suitable dog, and finally found an eighteen-month-old Papillon that had been returned to his breeder. Although a Papillon looks nothing like a Bearded Collie, when the younger Barbara placed

Andre in her mother's arms, she knew she had found the perfect match.

Andre lived with Barbara Allen and was her constant companion for twelve years. When Barbara moved in with her daughter in Bedford, Massachusetts, Andre accompanied her and settled in immediately. Three years later, however, Barbara fell and broke her hip. She moved into a nursing home, where Andre couldn't accompany her.

But he could still visit. Andre's little body would quiver with anticipation as the car rolled into the nursing home's drive. Barbara looked forward to these visits with the same excitement, often dressing in her favorite pink suit for the occasion. When Andre arrived, dog and owner shared an ecstatic reunion, complete with wet doggie kisses. After a few minutes, Andre settled into Barbara's lap, and she took him for a ride down the corridors in her wheelchair, searching out fellow patients to whom she could show him off. Andre greeted everyone cordially as long as he remained in the safety of Barbara's lap.

Finally, Barbara was rehabilitated enough to come home. Andre was thrilled to have his owner back and rarely left her side. Barbara's daughter hired a nurse, George, to care for her mother during the day while she was at work. Barbara would gather Andre onto her lap, and George would wheel the two of them out into the garden. George and Barbara would play cards or games while Andre remained curled up in Barbara's lap.

Andre and Barbara lived each peaceful day to the fullest, basking in each other's companionship until suddenly Barbara experienced a relapse. She returned to the hospital, where she died two days later.

Andre waited in vain for his owner to come back. Every day for the next month Andre went to the spot on the lawn where they had last been together and laid down.

Barbara's daughter says, "I had to pick him up and bring him in or I believe he would have stayed there forever."

Andre lived for another year and a half, although he never was the same, taking longer and longer naps, and often gazing into the distance as if remembering happier times. Every chance he had, he would steal away to the garden to wait for his mistress. Finally, he died of old age. Barbara believes that now, in death, her mother and Andre have finally been reunited.

"I'm sure they're watching from 'up there,'" Barbara insists. "Mom is in her smoky pink suit with Andre curled up in her lap."

APOLLO

Apollo the Great Dane was always a welcome sight at the Maple Leaf Nursing Home in New Hampshire. He knew every inch of the two-story building and would bound enthusiastically down the halls with his owner, Lyn Richards, in tow. Lyn and Apollo did therapy work at the home. Apollo knew which rooms were "his," and he would skid to a halt outside these doors, then drag Lyn in to see his patients.

His favorite patient was his best friend Eva Moore. Eva was 103 years old and measured a tiny 4'5", which put her on eye level with the Great Dane. They seemed to see eye-to-eye in many ways, as they would cuddle on the bed and Eva would share the secrets of her long and glorious life with her rapt audience.

One day, Apollo bounced into Eva's room on the second floor, but she was nowhere to be found. The Great Dane rushed to the bed, his nose sniffing eagerly for his friend. When he didn't find Eva there, he searched the floor, behind the nightstand, and in the closet. He looked everywhere, but Eva just wasn't there. Suddenly, his haunches sank to the floor and he sat with his head tilted back, letting loose a long, eerie howl that seemed to come from deep within his soul. Lyn tried frantically to calm him, but he continued to howl. As Lyn soothed him, the wail quieted, but was replaced by a heart-wrenching whimper. At that moment, the floor nurse ran into the room. She sat on the bed, as tears ran unchecked down her cheeks.

"It's okay boy, she knew you loved her," she reassured the mournful dog. "She's happier now." Apollo walked over to her and rested his great head in her lap. Lyn was amazed to see real tears filling her dog's eyes.

There is no doubt that Apollo not only felt grief, but also sensed the death of his wonderful friend even before his owner had realized she was gone.

Apollo continued his visits to Maple Leaf, and for a while Lyn would notice him turn his head as they neared Eva's room as if he were about to enter, then check himself and move on. The new resident in his old friend's room was a man who wasn't fond of dogs. Even if he were, it is hard to imagine he could have replaced Eva in Apollo's heart.

HEIDI

Graham Snell awoke one morning and decided to take a walk. But this was no stroll around the block. Graham set off with his Jack Russell Terrier, Heidi, to climb the 3,152-foot peak of Ben Klibreck in Scotland.

The duo made it about a third of the way up the mountainside when Graham slipped, plunging over the side of a steep cliff. One can only imagine the terror and helplessness Heidi felt as her master disappeared from sight. Still, somehow she managed to climb gingerly down the treacherous embankment to reach her owner's side. There was nothing she could do to revive him—Graham had been killed by the fall. Heidi curled up next to his lifeless body and waited.

Day passed into night, then day, then night again. Surely the little terrier was cold and hungry, but she remained there, guarding the body of her companion. Finally, with daybreak, came the sounds of a helicopter circling above. A Royal Air Force chopper discovered Graham about 1,200 feet up the mountain with his loyal friend beside him.

Heidi was taken to the Munlochy Animal Aid Center, where she was cared for until her owner's family arrived. After identifying their father's body, Graham's children came to collect Heidi and take her home to Berkshire, Scotland. The airline they had flown in on, however, refused to allow a dog on the flight.

Hearing of Heidi's plight, British Regional Airlines stepped in and generously agreed to fly Heidi home, accompanied by Ann Agnew, the airline's customer services manager. Once she was safely on the ground, Heidi was escorted to her new home with her owner's daughter; only a few houses from the home she used to share with Graham.

There is no doubt in my mind that dogs are capable of grief, as well as a whole range of emotions traditionally denied by science. The tales in this book describe dogs from coast to coast, and indeed around the globe, who show an amazing aptitude for emotion in their relationships with people and with other animals. The canines described here—from altruistic therapy dogs to canine medics, from service dogs who help the disabled to the heroes of September 11—all seem to be living proof of the awesome, wonderful compassion of dogs.

88